Joseph A. Schumpeter

The *Major Conservative and Libertarian Thinkers* series aims to show that there is a rigorous, scholarly tradition of social and political thought that may be broadly described as 'conservative', 'libertarian' or some combination of the two.

The series aims to show that conservatism is not simply a reaction against contemporary events, nor a privileging of intuitive thought over deductive reasoning; libertarianism is not simply an apology for unfettered capitalism or an attempt to justify a misguided atomistic concept of the individual. Rather, the thinkers in this series have developed coherent intellectual positions that are grounded in empirical reality and also founded upon serious philosophical reflection on the relationship between the individual and society, how the social institutions necessary for a free society are to be established and maintained, and the implications of the limits to human knowledge and certainty.

Each volume in the series presents a thinker's ideas in an accessible and cogent manner to provide an indispensable work for both students with varying degrees of familiarity with the topic as well as more advanced scholars.

The following twenty volumes that make up the entire *Major Conservative and Libertarian Thinkers* series are written by international scholars and experts.

The Salamanca School	Andre Azevedo Alves (LSE, UK) & Professor José Manuel Moreira (Porto, Portugal)
Thomas Hobbes	Dr R. E. R. Bunce (Cambridge, UK)
John Locke	Professor Eric Mack (Tulane, US)
David Hume	Professor Christopher J. Berry (Glasgow, UK)
Adam Smith	Professor James Otteson (Yeshiva, US)
Edmund Burke	Professor Dennis O'Keeffe (Buckingham, UK)
Alexis de Tocqueville	Dr Alan S. Kahan (Paris, France)
Herbert Spencer	Alberto Mingardi (Istituto Bruno Leoni, Italy)
Ludwig von Mises	Richard Ebeling (Trinity College)

Joseph A. Schumpeter	Professor John Medearis (California, Riverside, US)
F. A. Hayek	Dr Adam Tebble (UCL, UK)
Michael Oakeshott	Dr Edmund Neill (Oxford, UK)
Karl Popper	Dr Phil Parvin (Cambridge, UK)
Ayn Rand	Professor Mimi Gladstein (Texas, US)
Milton Friedman	Dr William Ruger (Texas State, US)
Russell Kirk	John Pafford
James M. Buchanan	Dr John Meadowcroft (King's College London, UK)
The Modern Papacy	Dr Samuel Gregg (Acton Institute, US)
Murray Rothbard	Gerard Casey
Robert Nozick	Ralf Bader (St Andrews, UK)

Of course, in any series of this nature, choices have to be made as to which thinkers to include and which to leave out. Two of the thinkers in the series—F. A. Hayek and James M. Buchanan—have written explicit statements rejecting the label 'conservative'. Similarly, other thinkers, such as David Hume and Karl Popper, may be more accurately described as classical liberals than either conservatives or libertarians. But these thinkers have been included because a full appreciation of this particular tradition of thought would be impossible without their inclusion; conservative and libertarian thought cannot be fully understood without some knowledge of the intellectual contributions of Hume, Hayek, Popper and Buchanan, among others. While no list of conservative and libertarian thinkers can be perfect, then, it is hoped that the volumes in this series come as close as possible to providing a comprehensive account of the key contributors to this particular tradition.

John Meadowcroft
King's College London

Joseph A. Schumpeter

John Medearis

Major Conservative and
Libertarian Thinkers
Series Editor: John Meadowcroft
Volume 4

continuum

NEW YORK • LONDON

Continuum International Publishing Group

The Tower Building
11 York Road
London SE1 7NX

80 Maiden Lane
Suite 704
New York NY 10038

www.continuumbooks.com

ISBN: 978-0-8264-3012-0

Library of Congress Cataloging-in-Publication Data
Medearis, John.
Joseph A. Schumpeter / John Medearis.
p. cm.—(Major conservative and libertarian thinkers; v. 4)
Includes bibliographical references and index.
ISBN-13: 978-0-8264-3012-0 (hardcover : alk. paper)
ISBN-10: 0-8264-3012-0 (hardcover : alk. paper)
1. Schumpeter, Joseph Alois, 1883–1950. 2. Economists—United States. 3. Evolutionary economics—History. I. Title. II. Series.

HB119.S35M48 2009
330.1–dc22
2008045232

Typeset by Newgen Imaging Systems Pvt Ltd, Chennai, India
Printed in Great Britain by the MPG Books Group, Bodmin and Kings Lynn

Contents

Series Editor's Preface

Joseph A. Schumpeter was born in the Austro-Hungarian Empire toward the end of the nineteenth century. He entered the University of Vienna, one of the world's premier institutions of learning, at the outset of the twentieth century. In 1911 he was appointed to a full professorship at the University of Graz, an appointment marked by a ceremony in which he shook hands with Emperor Franz Joseph, and gained entry to the academic elite of the empire. Seven years after that ceremony the Austro-Hungarian Empire collapsed; in the aftermath of the First World War the Emperor relinquished power in favour of a democratic constitution and the old regime broke apart into its constituent countries.

Perhaps it is unsurprising, then, that Schumpeter's work contains a powerful sense of the inevitably dynamic and often destructive social change: he was concerned with the rise of democracy and the fall of aristocratic regimes; he coined the phrase "creative destruction" to describe the development of capitalist economies driven by entrepreneurial innovation, and he wrote of his belief that capitalism could not survive the ascent of socialism.

In this sense Schumpeter shared the concerns of many conservative thinkers that seemingly established and secure social orders were in reality highly precarious and liable to be swept away by strong social and cultural currents with potentially pernicious consequences.

In this outstanding account of Schumpeter's life and work, John Medearis of the University of California, Riverside, sets out the central features of Schumpeter's social, economic, and political thought in the context of his remarkable life, and also brilliantly captures the subtleties and nuances of one of the most original and provocative thinkers of the twentieth century.

This volume makes a crucial contribution to the Major Conservative and Libertarian Thinkers series by setting out the thought of one of the most innovative contributors to this tradition. In presenting Schumpeter's wide-ranging thought in such an accessible and cogent form, Medearis has produced an outstanding volume that will prove indispensable to those relatively unfamiliar with Schumpeter's work as well as more advanced scholars.

John Meadowcroft
King's College London

Author's Preface

Some social theorists make their work look simple—but not Joseph Schumpeter. True, he wore his erudition lightly, leaving readers with the twin impressions of a naturally fertile mind and a gift for vivid prose. But social analysis after Schumpeter's fashion was complex, demanding and recurrently painful. It was, first, demanding because Schumpeter believed any good investigator had to know an astounding amount about a range of human sciences. "Latin paleography," he once wrote, with just a hint of exaggeration, "is one of the techniques of economic analysis" (Schumpeter [1954] 1994, 13). Social analysis was complex, as well, because societies were not controlled laboratories but open systems of competing tendencies and countertendencies working out their effects over long stretches of historical time. Finally, social analysis was at least potentially painful because the analyst and his or her store of knowledge did not stand outside of the world being analyzed but were very much a "product" of it (Schumpeter [1954] 1994, 34). One crucial facet of this unavoidable embeddedness was the analyst's social ties and political allegiances. Schumpeter himself provides an illustration. His writings display a very palpable sense of beliefs being affronted, valued things being threatened—in short, dismay at what his own investigations showed him about the direction of historical change. A scholarly survey of Schumpeter's thought, then, cannot help but portray a committed political thinker and the difficulties he faced—not always with success—in attempting to make sense of the often-tumultuous times in which he lived.

This way of putting things marks an unavoidable difference between this book and many other treatments of Schumpeter.

The characteristic view, adopted especially by scholars who admire a contribution of Schumpeter's to their particular field, is that he was a social scientist who just happened to have privately conservative political views. But the very aim of this volume is to understand Schumpeter as a conservative thinker. Although I have attempted throughout to represent a range of interpretations and uses of Schumpeter's writings this is one crucial sense in which such evenhandedness has proved intrinsically impossible.

Yet despite my necessarily atypical guiding theme, I have avoided emphasizing both distinctive interpretations of Schumpeter's work that I have articulated elsewhere and my own approaches to issues such as democracy or the state. I offer what I hope are some new and illuminating perspectives on Schumpeter's intellectual development and his place in social and political theory, while providing a broad intellectual portrait, and demonstrating both how and why an impressive range of scholars and intellectuals have recurrently come back to his work. The first chapter, then, lays out the often fascinating details of Schumpeter's life, but also argues that his conservatism was first shaped by the political dynamics of Austria-Hungary, where he was born. In particular, I argue that Schumpeter's view of conservatism as a matter of rearguard actions against powerful historical trends grew partly out of the common wisdom of those who most ardently defended the Habsburg dual monarchy until its demise in 1918. Because Schumpeter was so prolific and diverse in his output, the second chapter, a critical survey of his work, must cover a great deal of ground. But in it I also attempt to demonstrate precisely what it was about his written work (not just his private views) that marks him as a member of the family of conservatives—especially noting his analytical narrative of capitalist decline, his recurrently expressed skepticism about human reason, his critical examination of the role of intellectuals in social change, and his highlighting the role of elite leadership in all societies. Like the second chapter, the third, on Schumpeter's influence, is necessarily wide ranging, discussing scholars from feudal historians to theorists of business innovation. But I also argue there that the deepest frames and assumptions governing how Schumpeter has been read and used since his death were themselves shaped, and to some extent distorted, by crucial lags between the time and circumstances in which he formulated his views and the era in which his contributions were fully incorporated into the canon of social science. The last chapter argues that contemporary interpreters of Schumpeter—scholars and public intellectuals alike—confront a number of uncongenial elements in his work that are intimately connected to his most fruitful ideas, arguments, and analyses. These surpluses range from assumptions that undermine economic libertarianism, to the evidence of his anti-Semitism, to certain off-putting habits of thought and expression.

I could not have written this book without the inspiration, help, and comments of others. I was lucky enough to have two teachers, Carole Pateman and Richard Ashcraft, whose writings pointed me insightfully toward Schumpeter some years ago. I received two indispensable forms of support from the University of California, Riverside. The first was the opportunity to take a partial sabbatical to finish the manuscript. The second was financial assistance making it possible for me to hire a research assistant, Mayia Shulga, who did exemplary research and helped prepare the manuscript for publication. Jessica Goodheart, my wife, made helpful and generous comments on draft chapters, and even my son Max once or twice requested, to my surprise, that I read portions of the manuscript to him at bedtime in lieu of Sherlock Holmes.

John Medearis
University of California, Riverside

1

Life

The Shaping of a Young Austro-Hungarian Conservative, 1883–1913

Life stories, we might think, should begin with birthplaces. Yet to search for the origins of Joseph Schumpeter's thought in Triesch, the town where he spent the first four years of his life, while evocative is also speculative. For the fact is that Schumpeter's adult ties to Triesch were stretched thin by death, distance, and fading memory. He never attempted to explore his roots in the small town in the Czech-Moravian Highlands, so that we today probably have more precise information about his ancestors there than he ever did. His earliest years in Triesch were eventually so remote to the grown Schumpeter that in talking about his upbringing he sometimes confused the very names of his grandfather and unfortunate father. And yet the story of Schumpeter's separation from Triesch tells us a great deal about the person he would become and the country that shaped him.

In 1883, the year of Schumpeter's birth, Triesch was in the Czech-majority region of the vast, multiethnic Austro-Hungarian Empire, an unlikely political construction which was to rip apart when Schumpeter was still a young man. Austria-Hungary, one could say justly, was comprised of two kingdoms under a single Habsburg monarch, and about a dozen national groups, from Ukrainians to Italians, with Poles, Croats, and Czechs in between. But even so wordy a description as this does not do justice to the political and ethnic complexity of the sprawling empire. Rather than the solid ethnic blocks that maps of the empire sometimes seem to show, there were everywhere different demographic mixes, with different ethnic groups relating differently to each other. The ruling Habsburgs themselves, having governed places as far afield as Spain and the Netherlands, actually considered themselves to be above ethnic and national identifications. But throughout much of Austria-Hungary, for much of its history, those traders, lawyers, imperial officials, doctors, manufacturers, and army officers who most identified with the empire and not its centrifugal nationalities, usually spoke German and thought of themselves as German. Until very late in the history of the empire, German, Schumpeter's first language, was the language of the state, the language in which high officials spoke to each other, if not to the public.

From the early nineteenth century onward, this dominant position was under steady attack, not the least by Czechs. This multipronged nationalist challenge, the threat it posed to the Habsburg empire, and the imperial government's many responses, together constituted dominant themes of Austro-Hungarian politics for the century leading up to First World War. Yet other momentous sociopolitical changes were afoot in Schumpeter's youth, as well. The industrial revolution had come relatively late to Austria-Hungary, but it was well under way in 1883, when Schumpeter was born into a family whose wealth derived from the manufacturing of textiles. Industrialization and subsequent urban migration had fostered the growth of an increasingly powerful working-class movement, whose political expression was the Austrian Social Democratic Party (SDP). Schumpeter would come to be well aware of this working-class political challenge, living as he would later, just off Vienna's *Ringstrasse*, in a part of the capital where the party organized mass marches during the 1890s and 1900s.

The Schumpeter family's status, the significance of the economist's life trajectory, and his own political orientation all make sense only against this historical background. In the late nineteenth century, the Schumpeters were part of the local German-speaking minority of notables in Triesch and the surrounding region.[1]

Such Germans called the town Triesch, while the local Czechs called it Třešt'. In a bureaucratic compromise characteristic of the empire, the local postmark included both spellings (Shionoya 1989, 158). The economist's great grandfather, a master weaver, had built a horse-powered textile mill in 1832, then converted it to steam power (Allen 1991, 1: 9).[2] Although this lagged steam's introduction in England, it was a first in Triesch, and helped trigger a miniature industrial revolution there (Meissner 1979, 256). The grandfather, Alois Schumpeter, took over the factory and was mayor of the town for about seven years. The business role of the economist's father, Josef Alois Karl Schumpeter, is less certain because of his early death. Years later, it would have been natural for Schumpeter, the economist, to refer to his family's textile business in Triesch in his prominent writings on the proliferation of innovation, but he never did. And so, strangely, we cannot say with any certainty that the Schumpeter family's entrepreneurial past had an influence on the adult economist's interests. Indeed, it would be Jozsi (for that was the economist's boyhood name) who would break with family business tradition, finding a career and a life far from Triesch in every respect.

In large part, this break was the accomplishment of his mother, born Johanna Grüner, whose ambitions for Jozsi we must also view against the backdrop of the forces of fracture and centralization in Austria-Hungary. Though similarly regarding themselves as German, the Grüners' outlook was likely somewhat different from that of the Schumpeters of Triesch. While the Schumpeters were local notables and business people, the Grüners likely identified more strongly with the imperial civil service and more cosmopolitan professions. At the time of her birth, Johanna's father was a doctor in the imperial army, stationed not in Moravia, but in Wiener Neustadt, south of Vienna. Of all the institutions of Austria-Hungary, it was the giant army that was the most closely associated with the very person of the emperor and with the vast transnational empire. Joseph Roth's remarkable novel, *The Radetzky March* (1995), conveys this vividly in a witty but affecting tale of a Slovenian soldier of peasant stock who almost inadvertently saves the emperor's life at the Battle of Solferino and is rewarded by Franz Joseph with a military promotion and knighthood. The result is that he and his descendents are torn from their Slovenian roots, their fates yoked to empire and disastrously transformed. Just as portrayed in the novel, the army maintained garrisons in many towns—the most visible representatives of imperial power—and insisted that its officers use German as the language of command, regardless of the language of the local peoples. Though Schumpeter was never a soldier or officer, the imperial army would prove crucial in separating him from his origins in Triesch and placing him on a wider imperial stage. And this fact also foretells something of Schumpeter's first political allegiances, which would be to all the social forces and institutions that bound empire and emperor together.

Johanna's father, the army doctor, eventually moved from Wiener Neustadt back to the family's home of Iglau (Jihlava in Czech), a larger Moravian town near Triesch, in order to succeed his own father as director of the hospital there. Some years later, in 1881, Johanna was married in Iglau, then moved with her husband to Triesch. According to many accounts, she was highly conscious of both the Grüners' and Schumpeters' social status, which she likened, with considerable exaggeration, to that of aristocrats in the cities such as Vienna (Allen 1991, 1: 10). In notes for an unpublished autobiographical novel, Schumpeter later described a character very like his mother as an "excellent woman" who "had connections that she resolutely exploited for her darling" in order to make him a "gentleman."[3] It became clear when Jozsi was still young where his mother's ambition pointed and where she would find those connections.

For when the child was just four years old, his father was killed in an apparent hunting accident. Within a short time Johanna embarked on a remarkable course of action, propelling herself and her son toward the cultural, educational, and political center of Austria-Hungary, as well as toward aristocracy and empire—at a time when so many other social forces pulled the other way. She would make use of both the military's and higher education's roles in Austria-Hungary as tools for assimilation and transnational unity—tools by which the conservative powers of emperor and aristocracy absorbed and promoted talented members of the bourgeoisie. A little more than a year after her husband's death, Johanna took Jozsi to Graz, a small city about 200 kilometers south of Vienna, to which many military officers retired. There Johanna and her son lived alone while Jozsi went to school. But within five years Johanna married retired Field Marshal-Lieutenant Sigmund von Kéler. The match opened up great opportunities for her son. Although he had an ample pension, von Kéler was not rich. Yet the "von" in his name indicated membership in "second society," the lower aristocracy, many of whose members had been ennobled for military or bureaucratic service to the emperor. By virtue of his military rank, he would have been "*hoffähig*"—permitted to enter the imperial court (Johnston 1972, 40). And his rank entitled him to be addressed as "your Excellency," a distinction his new young wife would insist upon as well (Seidl 1984, 190 n. 24; Allen 1991, 1: 23). After marrying, Johanna and von Kéler moved with Jozsi to Vienna, where Schumpeter was able, probably through von Kéler's status and connections, to enroll in the Theresianum, a prestigious school generally reserved for aristocratic children. The Theresianum provided as good an education as anyone could obtain in the empire. Schumpeter, who had never learned Czech in Triesch, would come to be fluent in all the languages of the aspirationally cosmopolitan aristocracy—French, English, and Italian—as well as Latin and ancient Greek. At the Theresianum, Schumpeter would also become exposed to a particular aristocratic attitude of ironic detachment, an ability to understand and even temporarily adopt the points of view of different parties without actually identifying with them. This can easily be overstated—one should never doubt that Schumpeter had powerful conservative convictions—but most personal accounts suggest that this was nevertheless a pose Schumpeter could adopt at will.

Schumpeter apparently thrived at the Theresianum, which he attended from 1893 until 1901, the year he turned 18. Late in the fall of 1901, he entered the University of Vienna. Today, when higher education is in many places much more democratic, and professors are perhaps no more highly esteemed than they should be, it is somewhat difficult to imagine the exalted atmosphere of the University of Vienna. Both the Theresianum and the University occupied a special place in the empire. Such institutions, according to the historian Arno Mayer, were intended simultaneously to train and fill "the upper cadres of the civil service" and professions, and to "fuse the sons of bourgeois and middle-class families into the old ruling class on terms acceptable to the latter" (Mayer 1981, 254). Ambitious parents, then, educated their sons in such institutions in order to help them internalize "the ethos and life-style of landed and public service nobilities" (254). This appears to be exactly what Johanna aimed for and accomplished. The ties between the University of Vienna and imperial service were extremely close. A large number of students, as Mayer suggests, became civil servants upon graduation, and all faculty members were *de jure* civil servants themselves, whose official appointments required an audience with the emperor. (Schumpeter himself had such an audience some years later.) The most renowned professors were sometimes even made members of the *Herrenhaus* (House of Lords) for their service to science (Johnston 1972, 70). Others' service to Franz Joseph was more direct. Eugen von Böhm-Bawerk, the most famous of the economics professors during Schumpeter's years at the university, had served as the imperial minister of finance. Moreover, almost all such faculty saw themselves as contributing to policy debates, as well as to scientific ones. Although Schumpeter later in life insisted that one should never subordinate honest scientific inquiry to short-term political purposes—a point often stressed by his interpreters—we should not fail to recognize how the political connections and status of the University of Vienna must have reinforced the developing student's sense of allegiance to the emperor and instilled in him a powerful feeling that economics was an important calling.

In his university years, Schumpeter was able to profit from an education in which newer social-scientific ideas were introduced along with classical themes. He also had the chance to contend with some exceedingly sharp minds. There were, of course, his teachers. By the time he began to study economics, a new way of thinking, variously termed marginalism or neoclassical economics, had become the dominant mode. Its founders were Léon Walras, William Stanley Jevons, and Carl Menger, the last of whom had reigned and left his mark at the University of Vienna, but had retired while Schumpeter was still a school boy. In light of what I have said about the bonds between crown and gown discernible in Schumpeter's Vienna, it is worth noting that Menger had been an imperial civil servant and no ordinary one. He had tutored Franz Joseph's son, Crown Prince Rudolf, and traveled with him to England. As Schumpeter would be some years later, Menger and Rudolf had been deeply impressed by the social and political leadership they thought was provided by the English aristocracy, and, so inspired, they together wrote and published (anonymously) a volume titled *The Austrian Aristocracy and Its Constitutional Profession* (May 1965, 163; Johnston 1972, 35). Around the time of Schumpeter's matriculation, Menger was replaced by his leading follower, Friedrich von Wieser, from whom the student absorbed a great deal.

But no seminar seems likely to have captured Schumpeter's imagination more than the one led by Böhm-Bawerk in 1905–6. It developed into a sharp engagement over economic theory between the professor and certain students who were tireless advocates of capitalism, on one side, and another group of students who would become influential socialist leaders and thinkers, on the other. According to Allen, who himself took courses with Schumpeter decades later at Harvard, "Schumpeter was proud of having attended that seminar and spoke of it and of his favorite professor, Böhm-Bawerk, to his colleagues and students many times in later years" (1991, 1: 49, n. 12). Schumpeter supposedly refused to support either side for very long, making opportunistic attacks when he perceived intellectual weaknesses (Allen 1991, 1: 39–40; Haberler 1950, 338). If his later writings are a guide to his motivations at the time, this is likely not because of any sympathy for socialism (he had essentially none) but because he thought the Marxists were right about some of marginalism's weaknesses, especially its neglect of dynamism and historical change. The most intransigent defender of capitalism in the seminar was likely Ludwig von Mises, later a mentor to Friedrich von Hayek, and today a man regarded as an essential figure in the twentieth-century conservative canon. On the Marxist side was Rudolf Hilferding, who had written a response to Böhm-Bawerk's polemic against Marx's theory of surplus value.[4] (Hilferding eventually served briefly as finance minister of Weimar Germany, and years later died in a Gestapo prison in occupied Paris.[5]) Also taking part was Otto Bauer, author and SDP strategist, who would later serve alongside Schumpeter in the government of the Austrian Republic. And finally there was Emil Lederer, who held professorships in Germany before fleeing and establishing himself, along with other refugees, at the New School in New York. In this as in other ways, Schumpeter's university experience was not an escape from Austro-Hungarian political life but a potent distillation of it.

In 1906, Schumpeter graduated with a degree in law and embarked on a few years of travel and life abroad. His first stop was Berlin, where in the spring and summer he attended a seminar on political economy, and established contacts with renowned economists, especially those of the "historical school," whose leader was Gustav Schmoller. The historical school took part in a long-running intellectual battle with the economic marginalists, such as Menger. Schumpeter later regarded the battle as a waste of effort, and while he built his early economic work on marginalist concepts, he increasingly adopted a very historical approach to understanding the economy. After some time in Paris, Schumpeter next settled for about a year in England. There he was a research student at the London School of Economics, spending hours reading at the British Museum, and visiting with luminaries of English economics, such as Alfred Marshall. Marshall advised him not to pursue economics, according to Schumpeter's later account (1951, xi). He also found time to meet—and rather precipitously to marry—an older British woman named Gladys Ricarde Seaver, the daughter of an official in the Church of England. Little is really known about their marriage and its fairly rapid practical dissolution. (For some time, scholars even debated Gladys's age.) But the two had begun to live separately—he in Austria-Hungary and she in England—even before war broke out between their respective home countries in 1914, and the beginning of hostilities apparently made the break permanent. In contrast to the relative brevity of the marriage, one of the most lasting influences of Schumpeter's time in England may have been a view he developed of English politics as involving strong aristocratic leadership, which in his view blunted and absorbed democratic impulses for change. Strangely, this view of "Tory democracy" would seem mainly to be an interpretation of Victorian England—or more narrowly, the era of Gladstone and Disraeli—rather than of the Edwardian era he experienced personally.

In any case, not long after Joseph and Gladys's wedding, the couple moved to Cairo, where Schumpeter was able to practice law on the strength of his undergraduate degree, without further training. But by this time it seems clear that Schumpeter's intention was to make a career in economics, not law. How he found the time for the project is something of a mystery, but after a few months in Cairo, Schumpeter had finished a manuscript he had apparently begun in England: *The Nature and Essence of Theoretical Economics.* In October 1908, after returning to Vienna, he submitted this as his *Habilitationsschrift,* a sort of dissertation proving his ability to teach at the university level. This book was essentially a summary of the state of the economic theory he had absorbed in the last five years, and in particular a tribute to the French economist Léon Walras's mathematical approach to marginalism. Credential in hand, Schumpeter taught for a while in Vienna before moving with Gladys to take a position at the University of Czernowitz. It is yet another reminder of the size and diversity of the long-dead empire that Czernowitz—a small city in which Russians, Ukrainians, and Germans, Jews and Christians, all jostled each other—was nearly 1,000 kilometers east of imperial capital, and that today, known as Chernivtsi, it is part of Ukraine. There Schumpeter provoked the students with advanced economics and annoyed colleagues with Viennese affectations.

But more than anything he labored mightily to finish his next book. *The Theory of Economic Development* would turn out to be much that *Theoretical Economics* was not—pioneering where the earlier book had largely covered familiar ground, dynamic in focus where the earlier book had emphasized steady-state economics. In *Economic Development,* Schumpeter introduced many of the most important themes for which he is known. The book would also help make Schumpeter's career. And from the standpoint of Schumpeter's developing sociopolitical attitude, the book is important in that it presented a picture of what he most admired about capitalism: the innovation that set the economy in motion and constantly revolutionized it. In fact, in combination with the Tory democracy memos, which I discuss below, we can get from *Economic Development* a fairly complete sense of Schumpeter's political ideal: a society in which entrepreneurs propelled the capitalist economy on to new productive heights, while a traditional aristocracy, in firm control of the state, managed the strains of modern society with the self-assurance borne of centuries of domination.

Likely with Böhm-Bawerk's help, Schumpeter was appointed in 1911 to be full professor at the university in Graz, the city to which he had moved from Moravia nearly a quarter-century earlier, then just a child trailing his recently bereaved mother. The 28-year-old's return to Graz showed the distance he had traveled in between, from the fatherless provincial to the connected young professor with every prospect of participation in the academic and bureaucratic elite of the empire. Wearing a uniform special for the occasion, Schumpeter shook hands with the Emperor, Franz Joseph, in a ceremony marking the Graz appointment (Allen 1991, 1: 121).

Schumpeter kept his position at Graz for about ten years. Relatively early in this period, he wrote a book on the history of economics commissioned by the sociologist, Max Weber, eventually known in English as *Economic Doctrine and Method:*

An Historical Sketch. But, while it foreshadows his better known *History of Economic Analysis,* the book is not generally considered on a par with Schumpeter's classic texts. And what is most important about the Graz decade for us is Schumpeter's entrance into political life. The potential for such involvement, as I have suggested, was deeply inscribed in the academic institutions in which Schumpeter's career and public character had been formed, but it is clear that the immediate impetus was the First World War and the threat it posed to Austria-Hungary.

War, Fragmentation, and "Tory Democracy," 1914–18

After the emergence of a united Germany as a major power in the latter decades of the nineteenth century, Europe had eventually divided into a "Triple Alliance" of "Central Powers," including Germany, Austria-Hungary, and Italy, and a "Triple Entente" of France, Russia, and England. The Balkans, including parts of Austria-Hungary as well as the region to its southern borders, represented a particularly sharp clash of these blocs' interests. Slovenian and Croatian nationalists hoped for a Yugoslav state with Serbia as its core, but attainment of this goal would have deeply threatened the Austro-Hungarian empire. Russia had had a deep interest in the region, the historical locale of clashes between Orthodox Slavs and Muslim Turks, since at least the eighteenth century, with Pan-Slavs often expressing the wish for an empire or federation that would reach to the straits near Istanbul. After a member of a Serbian radical group, the "Black Hand," assassinated Archduke Franz Ferdinand in 1914, Austria-Hungary declared war on Serbia, receiving an unconditional promise of support from Germany. Russia went to Serbia's defense, and with an eye to members of the Alliance that could oppose this move, also mobilized along its border with Germany. Germany responded by declaring war on Russia, and then on France. England joined the war soon after. A conflict whose onset excited many subjects of the combatant nations soon developed into a pointless stalemate that generated only abundant, appalling casualties.

Differences between Austria-Hungary and its more powerful ally, Germany, developed throughout 1915. For Schumpeter, these differences came to a head with a secret German diplomatic note late that year, details of which he apparently learned of from a colleague. The communication demanded a favoring of German over Slav interests within Austria-Hungary that was at odds with the historical Habsburg attitude of indifference, even hostility, to ethnic nationalism. It also called for closer cooperation between Germany and the Habsburg empire, including a tariff or customs union between the two allied states.

It is undoubtedly the tariff proposal that provided Schumpeter with the opportunity to comment expertly on the note, but from the outset his concerns in doing so were broad, embracing the whole war and its implications for Austria-Hungary. The once-secret memos and letters that Schumpeter wrote from early 1916 to early 1918 are not numbered among his most influential and important writings, but they are invaluable guides to his political thinking at the time, demonstrating both his allegiance to monarchy and traditional Austro-Hungarian social relations, as well as his adoption of a type of conservative political wisdom shaped by Austro-Hungarian history. Schumpeter's counsel can be found in a series of letters to Heinrich Lammasch, a teacher of Schumpeter's who eventually was prime minister in the last imperial government, and to Count Otto Harrach, a deeply conservative high aristocrat, as well as in a set of memos Schumpeter intended to be circulated in conservative, aristocratic circles.

Schumpeter announced his overall concerns in the opening sentences of the first memo, in which he contended that the war affected the Austro-Hungarian monarchy differently and more seriously than other participating states. All the combatants were impoverished by the war. "[B]ut only the Monarchy will be disturbed also in its entire domestic structure," he wrote, adding "only [the Monarchy] experiences a complete shift of the elements of its existence and position" (Schumpeter [1916]

1985, 251). Politics, not just economic policy, would be his subject—and the Habsburg monarchy his chief concern, not any watery general conception of the good of the peoples of Austria-Hungary. He appealed to "that Austria that we know and love," a phrase that especially signified not a nation—Austria was not a nation, after all—but rather an interrelated set of social relations: "all those factors in which the true being and essence of Austria pulses, the All-High Imperial House, the historical [aristocratic] families, the special Austrian sense of parties and groups" (262). In fact, Schumpeter stressed over and over in these letters and memos his inclination to view all issues through the lens of such traditional institutions, most of all the monarchy (Schumpeter [1916–18] 1992, 364, 366, 368).

Schumpeter was convinced that a customs union with Germany would have been deeply threatening to such institutions. Indeed, his frank subordination of free trade principles to dynastic interests is striking in an economist of his training. After a customs union, he argued, many Austrian industries that were weaker than their German counterparts would disappear (Schumpeter [1916] 1985, 254). And as in industry, so in finance: weaker Austrian banks would lose out to Berlin banks—a loss made dangerous by the fact that the latter banks were subordinate to the German regime (256–7). Because German trade was far more important for Austria-Hungary than Austro-Hungarian trade was for Germany, the relationship would be a starkly unequal one (255). Austria-Hungary would become dependent upon Germany—a mere "economic province of Germany" (255). And crucially, all this would spell a loss of political autonomy for the monarchy (261).

Schumpeter's letters and memos were by no means limited, however, to providing reasons for resisting the customs union. But to understand the broader program he suggested it is necessary to understand a bit more of his view of the society he lived in than can be gleaned from the texts at hand. Writing almost thirty years later, in *Capitalism, Socialism and Democracy,* Schumpeter would make a strong claim that up until the First World War, European societies were still led by their aristocracies, and not by the bourgeois classes who were revolutionizing European economies. The aristocracies, he believed, had traditions of political action, inherited wisdom and skill, and the instinctive respect of the masses—all accumulated since the feudal era, when they had risen to power on the strength of their ability to afford vulnerable European communities a novel form of military protection. Since the 1980s, a historical literature has arisen supporting a version of this argument: the view that during the nineteenth century, usually considered to be an era of Enlightenment ideals and bourgeois dominance, European aristocracies and other traditional or premodern social forms and ideologies actually proved remarkably resilient. Interestingly, one of the first scholarly proponents of this argument, Arno Mayer, was himself profoundly influenced by Schumpeter—as he notes in his *Persistence of the Old Regime* (Mayer 1981, 11–12, 133). According to Mayer, the "'premodern' elements were not the decaying and fragile remnants of an all but vanished past but the very essence of Europe's incumbent civil and political societies" (5–6). And another historian, Arthur J. May has captured well the political ethos of this aristocratic dominance in Schumpeter's native land:

> Austrian nobles were taught and believed profoundly that they were born to rule and that their set alone, as for centuries past, was fit to monopolize politics. It was impossible for them to reconcile their inherited convictions with the growth of popular participation in public affairs. As a class, the nobility venerated the existing social order, espoused conservative causes and reactionary policies, and allied themselves with the clerical forces. (May 1965, 160)

It is really only in light of such an ethos that we can understand Schumpeter's wartime memos and letters. For Schumpeter both appealed to an audience that held this view of aristocracy's pivotal importance and—after years at the Theresianum and the University of Vienna—shared it himself. Thus the core of the memos and letters was an attempt to try to rally the

Austro-Hungarian aristocracy to form a conservative political party that could lead the empire under modern political conditions, thereby extending the lease of the old regime. It was clear, he wrote, that "the rallying of Austria can be accomplished only by its historical families" (Schumpeter [1916] 1985, 269). There was no other group besides the high aristocracy in which "the Austrian sense of state pulses so exclusively and in which the tradition of dealing with the tasks of state is so lively" (269). Thus a "grand seigneur" would have to be plucked from high aristocratic circles for the job (269). The key challenge for this unnamed aristocratic leader would be to combat the "disorganization of all political will" (269) through the skillful leadership of session of parliament. Parliament would meet to pass a specific legislative program, including measures for dealing with war debts. But what was truly crucial was a parliamentary demonstration of loyalty to the imperial house (267). This, not specific legislative policy, was what could rescue Austria-Hungary from the dangers lurking in a customs union. Various government ministers would have to play a role in the parliamentary session, not merely to explain imperial policy but to win support for it (270). Such a session, if carried out properly, would "strengthen the domestic authority of the government" and "give the conservative circles a basis of support in the voting masses" (Schumpeter [1916–18] 1992, 362). Besides the plan for a parliamentary session, Schumpeter argued that a new conservative party led by aristocrats needed a conservative newspaper as its voice. Such an organ would "make the modern political technique of dominating public opinion serve old Austrian ideas and interests."[6]

In sum, Schumpeter was promoting a program he called "Tory democracy": "that technique of public life which has been perfected in England and which even in periods of sharpest democratic tendencies has preserved the influence of the aristocracy and generally of conservative interests."[7] In one important sense he was not merely repeating the common wisdom of the Austro-Hungarian aristocracy back to its leading members. True, he was giving voice to an agreed-on belief in the high aristocracy's political importance. But he was also suggesting more pointedly that it use its traditional prestige and inherited skill and power in a new way, to dominate new political realms, especially public debate, representative institutions and elections. By contrast, many aristocrats continued to see matters of state as almost private affairs of the emperor and imperial bureaucracy. Count Karl Stürgkh, "another bureaucrat who became Prime Minster" (Taylor 1942, 269)—had actually closed down parliament for the war. True to his later explicit descriptions of conservatism as involving the management—never the prevention—of change, Schumpeter was arguing that ignoring the proliferating institutions of democratic power would never succeed. These historical tendencies had to be managed and mastered, not shunned.

Along with this Tory democracy program, Schumpeter suggested a variety of measures that he thought would help channel and alleviate nationalist ambitions within the empire. For example, he expressed the hope that a coronation ceremony for the new Emperor, Karl, in Prague might help reconnect Czechs to the empire (Schumpeter [1916–18] 1992, 370). It is easy from our standpoint, knowing that the empire did tear apart at the end of the war, to see in such a proposal a naive underestimation of the power of nationalism. But of course, Schumpeter probably did not mean that a ceremony alone would suffice. Rather, he likely hoped that granting Czechs something like the status that Hungarians already enjoyed—an autonomous kingdom under Habsburg rule—would meet nationalist demands. Such an idea had been floated by Czechs fifty years earlier, and had been revived in 1917 by one of Karl's ministers, though Czech leaders were no longer interested (May 1965, 51; 1966, 649–50). And attempts at accommodation much like it had been the stuff of imperial politics for a century. In fact, Schumpeter's conservatism, in its determination to manage change without any hope of entirely preserving a cherished past—maintaining the empire by granting concessions to increasingly powerful national groups, sustaining aristocratic rule by dominating, not spurning emergent popular politics—seems to have partaken deeply of the spirit of Habsburg statecraft. Just after the war, Schumpeter would write: The "highest type of Conservative policy consists in refusing to shrink from the great necessities of the day, and instead seizes upon them realistically and constructs Conservative successes on what would otherwise have become Conservative defeats" (Schumpeter [1918–19] 1991, 144). Taylor has described Habsburg political wisdom very similarly:

> To be on the verge of ruin had been the experience of the Habsburgs from the beginning . . . and it was this familiarity with impending doom which enabled the Habsburgs to meet successive dangers, if not with wisdom, at any rate with calm persistence. They could say of their position, "hopeless, but not serious," long before the phrase became the keynote of Austrian politics. (Taylor 1942, 2)

In the Tory democracy memos, Schumpeter's tone was determined and cautiously optimistic, yet outspoken about the risks to "the Austria that we know and love." For the next thirty years, his political thought would always be structured by an appreciation for what he wanted to conserve, on the one hand, and a careful analysis of everything that threatened it, on the other. Over time, however, the determined tone of the memos would come to be replaced by a more resigned one whose distillation could easily be "hopeless, but not serious."[8]

Conservatism after the Old Regime: Ventures Political, Commercial, and Scholarly, 1919–32

At the end of the war it would in fact transpire that the situation of the monarchy was at last truly hopeless. Soon after Emperor Karl decreed the transformation of Austria into a federal union, the supposed parties to this union—Czechs, Ukrainians, and others—began to run their affairs as *de facto* autonomous national governments. Under these nationalist pressures, as well as demands for a democratic—or at least republican—constitution, Karl abdicated. American policy, strongly favoring self-determination for some ethnicities, put the seal on the empire's fate.

The end of the Austro-Hungarian old regime must have been a very bitter disappointment to Schumpeter. From 1918 on, his conservatism would always lack the firm anchor it had found in old regime elites and institutions. Schumpeter would continue to be suspicious of popular politics. He would perceive many of the same political imperatives—leaders who could steer society through gales of social change, who could unify and even form "political will." But it would be difficult to know to whom his political arguments appealed—what social group he thought could heed his counsel and take on the leadership role the old European aristocracy had so recently occupied. Certain aspects of his political thinking, it is true, would become more clearly articulated and developed. He would develop a theory of rationalization and politics, for example. And in the coming years he would renew and even deepen his belief that dynamic capitalism, though endangered, was worthy of some form of protection even when there were no more "grand seigneurs" to be recruited for the job. But he would begin to doubt the protection would be effective forever. In "The Crisis of the Tax State," written in the year of the empire's collapse, Schumpeter predicted for the first time that socialism would eventually replace capitalism in the West, a view he would amplify until his death. His public political writings after this point would always convey more than anything his restless, biting criticism of modern sociopolitical developments, and his private ruminations a despairing hunt for something, anything, that could preserve the few remaining institutions, beliefs, and practices he valued.

And yet, although he must have experienced the empire's fall as sudden and dislocating, Schumpeter landed on his feet. Early in 1919, he received an invitation from Hilferding and Lederer, his former fellow students at the University of Vienna, to be a member of the German Socialization Commission. Economic plans that went under the name "socialization" proliferated at the end of the war. Many had little to do with the core meaning of the term: transferring ownership of factories and other means of production to the state or to other "social" institutions. In fact, leaders of the German SDP, which came to power at the end of the war, actually had little enthusiasm for undertaking any kind of "socialization" that altered control of industry. Under considerable pressure from working-class activists, the government did form the commission to study socialization of the coal industry. But leaders had actually decided on a course of action—essentially to build on wartime economic planning and existing cartelization but to leave control in the hands of private industry—well before the commission ever issued its recommendations. Schumpeter, probably unaware of this *fait accompli*, accepted the invitation to join the commission and boarded a train for Berlin.

Discussion of his role there in the ensuing weeks has often turned unhelpfully on the question whether he was sympathetic to socialism or, on the contrary, remained a loyal proponent of capitalism. Schumpeter never adopted or believed in any of the normative underpinnings of socialism. But, as we shall see in later chapters, he did come to believe that a form of socialism was likely to supplant capitalism in the West, irrespective of what he and others desired. In 1919, Schumpeter seems already to have reached this conclusion. Nevertheless, he thought that socialism's time was still far off, and that the most Germany could attempt at war's end was limited experiments in economic crisis management. Some of his oft-cited comments in Berlin seem connected to his apparently detached interest in seeing such experiments undertaken (Allen 1991, 1: 163–5). But more broadly, as a commission member, it appears that Schumpeter chiefly focused on arguing for preserving "leadership" in socialized industry, as against demands for democratization (Stolper 1985).[9]

It was while he was in Berlin that Schumpeter received another invitation—to become finance minister of the new Austrian republic. The coalition government there was led by the Austrian SDP, but included ministers from the Christian Social Party, which had won nearly as many seats in the February 1919 elections. (The Christian Social Party, which had its origins among lower-middle-class Viennese voters, would become in the interwar years the political home of clerics, big business, army officers, and peasants.) Schumpeter likely appeared an acceptable finance minister to the SDP because he had advocated a "capital levy," a tax to be collected not in cash but in the form of stocks, bonds, and other such assets. Here there was probably a misunderstanding. Both Schumpeter and the socialists viewed this as a way to deal with the debts and destruction that were the legacy of the war, but some SDP leaders also saw it as a possible route to socializing certain industry sectors. This would be a source of friction. Schumpeter's tenure as finance minister was neither long nor marked by great accomplishments. The economic problems were clear: devastation and hunger compounded by inflation. He produced a "finance plan" that focused on the capital levy and on encouraging foreign investment in Austria.[10]

But as finance minister Schumpeter was unable to gain the support of the rest of the government, and antagonized a substantial segment of the public, as well, with remarks that seemed to indicate an inability to empathize with widespread suffering. He also annoyed SDP leaders, especially Otto Bauer, by seeming to pursue an autonomous foreign policy, contacting foreign diplomats to undermine the idea of closer ties between the new nation of Austria—the largely German-speaking rump of the old empire—and Germany itself (Swedberg 1991b, 62; März 1981, 170–2; Low 1974, 207–8). Bauer also suspected Schumpeter of scheming to block the government's plan to socialize the largest Austrian steel concern. Lastly, although his fellow government ministers may not have known about it, Schumpeter agreed to lend secret support to aristocratic plotters who stole currency from the Hungarian embassy and wanted to overthrow the short-lived Hungarian Soviet (Stolper 1994, 18–20). (Although the Soviet was a threat to Austria, entanglement in such a coup would have been reckless for the fragile Austrian coalition government.) In October, 1919, after only seven months as finance minister, he was dismissed.

The next six years of Schumpeter's life look to the intellectual biographer like drift. Schumpeter taught briefly again at the University of Graz, then finally resigned his position there in 1921. Supporters in the Christian Social Party who thought he had been unfairly treated saw to it that Schumpeter received a lucrative banking concession, which allowed him to work for several years as a sort of private fund manager until, in the Austrian economic crisis of 1924, his investments were wiped out. Yet the wholly negative judgment of this period—even Schumpeter termed it his "gran rifiuto" or "great waste"—is something of a retrospective construction. Prior to the crash, Schumpeter probably felt himself to be something of a business success, controlling sizeable investments and drawing a direct salary that McCraw (2007, 106) estimates at about $250,000 in contemporary dollars. It was the events of 1926, a year that seemed at first to mark a new start for Schumpeter, that quite naturally color our view of the broader period so darkly.

In the aftermath of his banking failure, when Schumpeter most needed a professional break, he actually got it, in the form of a job offer from the University of Bonn. In the fall of 1925, he moved into a large house in that German city and took up his position as professor of public finance. In short order, he married Annie Reisinger, a woman twenty years his junior.[11] Schumpeter hid her true background from his Bonn colleagues, and eventually told friends he had met her as a young girl, paid for her education in France and Switzerland, and then dated and married her when she came of age. This story—odd to an early twenty-first-century audience but perhaps tinged with romance for those who first heard it—was not true, though some of it made its way into a few of Schumpeter's earliest obituaries. Annie was in fact the daughter of the concierge in his mother's building in Vienna. For a few months beginning in 1920—when Annie was 17—she and Schumpeter went on a few dates. Five years later, in the aftermath of Schumpeter's banking failure, the two began seeing each other again. He proposed in May, 1925. There seems little doubt that Schumpeter loved Annie sincerely and deeply. But because Schumpeter, a Catholic, had never divorced Gladys Seaver, remarriage was complicated. Schumpeter had to rely on the socially tolerant attitude of the socialist municipal government in Vienna for a divorce, and then convert to Lutheranism to get married. The year following their marriage, Annie became pregnant. But whatever hopes and plans she and Schumpeter had sketched out for a future family life were to remain wretchedly unfulfilled. Just before Annie's due date, Johanna, Schumpeter's mother, died. And then, shockingly, both Annie and the baby died shortly after delivery, Annie of severe hemorrhaging that had begun some months earlier. Schumpeter never truly recovered from the three deaths that year. He was always melancholic, indeed probably depressive, and developed the habits of copying from and annotating Annie's diary, as well as writing out prayers, pleas and thanks addressed to her and to his mother. Not only this, but for the rest of his life the grim but undaunted worldview that characterized his young adult years would more often appear bitter and angry.

Schumpeter ultimately spent seven years in Bonn. For some of this time, his intellectual production was slowed by the need to earn money to pay back his banking debts. To this end, he gave numerous paid speeches to trade groups and similar organizations, a necessity he began to despise. He put a great deal of effort into a book on the theory of money, but felt he had been upstaged by John Maynard Keynes's publication of *A Treatise of Money* in 1930. He put the unfinished manuscript away for years (he did not apparently burn it, as he told some acquaintances) and it was published posthumously (Schumpeter 1970).

Despite the personal heartbreaks and professional hindrances of the Bonn years, the broader period beginning in 1918 and ending with Schumpeter's move to the United States in 1932 encompasses some of his most fruitful work in economic sociology, a field that involves not just economic phenomena in the narrowest sense, but also the cultural, social, and political institutions and practices surrounding, conditioning, and interacting with such phenomena. I have already mentioned "The Crisis of the Tax State," which views the capitalist economy not in isolation but in historical relation to the development of the state since feudal times. "The Sociology of Imperialisms" (1919) attempts to explain forcible expansion by states, at a time when the leading such explanation attributed this politico-military phenomenon to economic causes. And "Social Classes in an Ethnically Homogenous Environment" attributes the formation and durability of elite social groupings to the functions they fulfill for society. And Schumpeter produced other, less-celebrated examples of economic sociology during the period. For example, his essay "The Socialist Possibilities of Today," offered a theory of revolution according to which the road from existing capitalism to democratic socialism could be paved by the widespread creation of elected workers' councils within factories and other workplaces.[12]

The dozen years Schumpeter spent in banking and teaching at Bonn were marked by violent conflict and the growing power and radicalization of right-wing movements in both Germany and Austria.[13] More particularly, between the end of First World War and Schumpeter's arrival in Bonn, "Weimar" Germany had already experienced: an attempted communist rebellion; two right-wing coup attempts, including Adolf Hitler's "Beer Hall Putsch"; the assassination of a liberal cabinet minister by a conspiracy of military officers; hyperinflation; and partial foreign occupation to guarantee the payment of war reparations. The first years of Schumpeter's professorship in Bonn, however, generally coincided with a period of relative calm in German affairs.[14] Not so the last two years. Depression hit Germany particularly hard. Chancellor Heinrich Brüning, with the support of President Paul von Hindenburg, attempted from 1930–2 to aid the economy with unpopular policies, especially social welfare cuts, which were imposed by decree because he could not get the support of a parliamentary majority. German democracy, never popular with many groups in political society, was thus already in deeply trouble before Hitler's rise to power. During the frequent elections of this two-year period, support for the Nazi party grew steadily. Schumpeter did not join the Nazi party himself, but in his farewell speech to his Bonn students in July, 1932, he referred to it as "a monster of infinite impulse," a "colossus" that might be "counseled properly in economics" by a young economist, yielding "enormous subjective individual possibilities."[15] And in his diary, around the same time, he wrote: "what I feel in my innermost self is around Hitler," although he immediately asked: "But is it really so?" (Allen 1991, 1: 288). And such feelings apparently did not dissipate when Schumpeter took a position at Harvard.

Conservatism after the Old Regime: New Continent, New Contentions, 1932–50

After a pair of long visits to Harvard, Schumpeter finally accepted a permanent position there in 1932. He left Bonn for Cambridge, Massachusetts in September of that year. It is surely from his Harvard years that we derive a certain stereotypical image of Schumpeter: the mordant wit, the self-admitted and only slightly self-deprecating snob, the teller of tales, many exaggerated, others self-aggrandizing. Readers may in fact be surprised not to have encountered this famous Schumpeter earlier in this biographical narrative. But it is fairly clear that this Schumpeter was something of a self-conscious pose, and a pose about which we have the most evidence from his Harvard years, although it is likely Schumpeter began cultivating it earlier. John Kenneth Galbraith, the influential economist, met Schumpeter when he taught at Harvard in the 1930s. And his personal recollection of Schumpeter, recorded nearly five decades later, is probably as concise a summary as one can find of the Austrian's public persona at the time:

> He had an amused and expressive face and an unremitting love for company and conversation. That Cambridge lacked the style of Franz Josef's Vienna he never doubted, but he was

> determined to compensate as best he could. He held court each afternoon at a small coffee shop across Massachusetts Avenue from Widener Library; to his classes he recurrently pictured himself as man of sophisticated knowledge and worldly interests and also of frustrated ambition. He had intended as a young man, he said, to be the greatest scholar, the greatest lover and the greatest general of his generation, but sadly the circumstances of postwar Austria had denied him the possibility of a military career. A gentleman, he once told his impecunious graduate students—the figure is firm in my memory—could not live on less than $50,000 a year. That, taxes and prices considered, would be the approximate present equivalent of $300,000. Given the choice between being right and being memorable, Schumpeter never hesitated. (Galbraith 1981, 49)

Schumpeter constructed this classic self-portrayal in part from mischaracterizations and embellishments about his past which not only exaggerated some details but also hid other crucial ones from view. He claimed falsely that his stepfather, Sigmund von Kéler had commanded the Vienna military garrison (Allen 1991, 1: 29 n. 31). He boasted at Cambridge cocktail parties that years earlier, as a 26-year-old temporary professor, he had strolled late into his first faculty meeting at the University of Czernowitz wearing jodhpurs and complaining that the meeting time conflicted with his riding schedule (1: 96, 113 n. 2). In general, one can say of this cultivated image that it highlighted personal eccentricities while obscuring both private anguish and revelatory historical, political, and social facts. Perhaps most importantly for us, Schumpeter almost never discussed his political activities during and after First World War, and although everyone knew he was conservative, he managed to hide just how important politics had often been to him.

In moving to the United States, of course, Schumpeter did not escape the broadest social and economic trends that were buffeting Germany, although these played out in politics differently on the West side of the Atlantic. Schumpeter arrived in the fall of 1932 and moved into an apartment in the home of Frank Taussig, who was also a widowed economics professor. The Great Depression was well under way in the United States—indeed, it had deepened the previous year. Neither of the two leading candidates for the US presidency that year had promised any concrete large-scale initiatives to counter the severe economic slide. But just a few months after Schumpeter arrived in Cambridge, President Franklin Delano Roosevelt and the new Congress began to enact a set of programs that came to be known as the "first New Deal." Its centerpieces were aid for the millions of unemployed; the reorganization and regulation of banking; a system of agricultural production controls and subsidies; and state-sanctioned industrial self-regulation and cartelization.[16] Although Schumpeter believed that the failing economy could essentially right itself (Schumpeter 1934), and remained always convinced that government policy under capitalism should aim at freeing rather than constraining entrepreneurs, he was not quite as opposed to all of this as one might expect. He actually favored a massive emergency economic stimulus, a position that distinguished him significantly from many American business opponents of the New Deal (Allen 1991, 2: 21; Haberler 1981, 77 n. 16). But one clause of an early piece of New Deal legislation attempting to establish collective bargaining rights for workers appeared to concern Schumpeter deeply. Or rather, it was the American labor movement's use of the section that troubled him, since the clause itself proved legally ineffective and the legislation was overturned by the Supreme Court.[17] The clause provided a considerable ideological boost—the apparent support of the US president—to union organizing. This, along with the hardships faced by workers and the temporary delegitimization of business resulting from economic collapse, gave rise to a new round of labor activism and strife in the United States. In 1934, the same year that saw a civil war in Austria that ended with the Christian Social government shelling a working-class housing project, several US cities were hit with massive strikes, culminating in a general strike in San Francisco, sparked by a battle between dockworkers and police thereafter known as "Bloody Thursday."

Schumpeter regarded such events as signs of capitalism's social, cultural, and political disintegration—as effects of "rationalization" that undermined traditional forms of authority needed for capitalism's survival. He deplored strikes and unionization, which he saw as the illicit extensions of democracy to economic institutions, and symptoms of the decline of valuable premodern hierarchies. He lamented the inability of the American bourgeoisie to mount effective opposition to this change—in short to exhibit the sort of political leadership he had always seen as characteristic of European aristocracies. And he was rankled by what he saw as a shift in the allegiances of intellectuals toward forces and institutions of social reconstruction, especially their willingness to staff New Deal bureaucracies. In lectures delivered in 1941, Schumpeter looked back and summed up the years immediately following his arrival in the United States. The "instability of capitalism" had become clear much earlier in Europe, he argued.

> The situation, then, in 1932–1933 was this. Of all the countries, America was the only country that was left and America had failed. We have this reduction of the prestige of businessmen in this country just as we observe in France of the eighteenth century after the battle of Rossbach. French society of the time existed on the basis of its military glory and leadership as the glory of America's society rests upon its business leadership. That society, as this one, also was being decayed anyway. We have complete disorganization in 1933, a complete disbelief in standards, a disbelief both in the old social relationships and in the new ones; there was moral rift. (Schumpeter [1941] 1991, 361)

Similar comments may be found as well in the most celebrated book of Schumpeter's American years, *Capitalism, Socialism and Democracy*, where Schumpeter specifically criticized New

Deal labor legislation establishing collective bargaining rights as "incompatible with the effective management of industry" (Schumpeter [1942] 1976, 161); criticized the "hired business executive" who "concludes that it is more pleasant to be commended for progressiveness—or to go on holiday—than to incur obloquy or danger by doing what nobody admits to be his duty," namely battling unions (214); and scorned the intellectual who "must flatter, promise and incite, nurse left wings and scowling minorities, sponsor doubtful or submarginal cases, appeal to fringe ends, profess himself ready to obey—in short behave toward the masses as his predecessors behaved toward their ecclesiastical superiors, later toward princes and other individual patrons, still later toward the collective master of bourgeois complexion" (154).

By 1932, when he began to teach at Harvard, Schumpeter had not published a major book for eighteen years.[18] But in the subsequent eighteen years, before his death in 1950, he wrote three significant ones. The first of these was *Business Cycles: A Theoretical, Historical and Statistical Analysis of the Capitalist Process* (1939). In writing it, Schumpeter intended to elaborate upon the main thesis of his *Theory of Economic Development*—that it was innovation that provided the engine of capitalist motion. Schumpeter's ambition to complement that theoretical claim with historical detail about the types of innovation that had marked capitalist development at different periods since the eighteenth century, as well as his attempt to resolve capitalist motion mathematically into a wavelike series of prosperous times and recessions, guaranteed, however, that the work would be laborious and his progress on the book far slower than he hoped.

During the late 1930s, he also worked periodically on ideas that would become *Capitalism, Socialism and Democracy*, which he did not actually publish until after the United States entered Second World War.[19] This is by far Schumpeter's most widely read and praised work, cited especially for the evocative term "creative destruction," a description of the results of innovation in a dynamic capitalist economy—as well as for the chapters on democracy, which, perhaps more than any other of his writings, continue to be cited by active scholars.

As early as the 1930s and throughout the 1940s, Schumpeter seems to have intended to write a new book on economic theory, one perhaps more mathematical than his *Theory of Economic Development*. But he made little headway, and other projects constantly pulled him away. For the rest of the war years and until his death in early 1950, Schumpeter spent a substantial amount of his time researching and writing the posthumously published *History of Economic Analysis*. In addition to comprising an impressive compendium of economic thought, this volume also contains some of Schumpeter's most interesting mature reflections on the nature and method of social science. In it Schumpeter explained more clearly than almost anywhere else what he meant by "economic sociology" and what he thought about its place in economic thinking. The book was also something of a distillation of years of reflection and research, for he likely drew on discussions he had had as early as the seminar of 1905–6. And he may also have made use of notes taken in the British Museum during his first trip to England. On the whole, it was solitary work, much of it performed in the Kress Library at the Harvard Business School.

Indeed, the intervals of hermetic research coincided with a kind of political isolation that resulted from Schumpeter's response to the Second World War. But this is best explained in light of his third marriage. When he had left Bonn in 1932, he had left behind a love affair—though at the time, it was not clear that the parting would be permanent. The year after Annie's death, Schumpeter had become involved with his housekeeper and secretary, Mia Stöckel. The relationship persisted even after Schumpeter moved to Cambridge, with the two meeting during the summers for several more years, but Schumpeter seems not to have seriously considered marrying Stöckel.[20] In the mid-1930s, however, he had met and begun to date Elizabeth Boody Firuski, an American economist whose expertise was in trade and the Japanese economy. Their correspondence suggests that she pursued him resolutely despite his depression and his continued quasi-religious devotion to his mother and his second wife, Annie. They married in 1937 and thereafter lived together, sometimes in Cambridge and sometimes in her home in rural Connecticut.[21]

For different reasons, the couple's opinions and scholarly interests made them objects of mistrust once the United States entered Second World War. The US Federal Bureau of Investigation suspected, because of Elizabeth's writings on the strength of the Japanese economy, that she was disloyal (Allen 1991, 2: 93–4). The bureau was apparently less worried about Schumpeter, although some of his public statements clearly suggested a desire not to oppose Nazi Germany. In particular, in a 1939 speech that received newspaper coverage, Schumpeter seemed to propose accepting many of Germany's aims (2: 93). Later, in his 1941 lecture series, he suggested that a future in which Germany dominated Europe would be acceptable (Schumpeter [1941] 1991, 388). Although the idea that Schumpeter would have presented a security risk to his adopted country seems preposterous, there is in fact considerable evidence that behind these public statements was a more general sympathy for Nazi Germany. We have already seen that, while Schumpeter never joined the Nazis, in his farewell speech in Bonn in 1932 he expressed fascination with the party, and support for the idea of a young economist seeking to advance his career by advising it—this, years after the publication of *Mein Kampf*. Similarly, even after Hitler became chancellor, took dictatorial powers, suppressed civil liberties, and arrested opponents, Schumpeter still was anxious not to be seen as a critic of Nazism (Schumpeter 2000, 243, 253). So while he participated at that point in efforts to help scholars, especially Jews, who fled Germany after Hitler took power, he did not want to be part of any effort that could be construed as a "general protest" against the Nazis and their rise to power (253). And at war's end, he raged against what he saw as a Bolshevik and "Jewish" victory (Swedberg 1991b, 150).

In addition to the sympathy with Nazi Germany, disturbing prejudices emerged during this period. To begin with, he recorded in his diary in 1941 his "hate against Russia" (Allen 1991, 2: 103). Contemporary audiences may not find a conservative economist's dislike of a communist country surprising. But economic doctrinal differences are probably not sufficient to explain Schumpeter's attitude. There is evidence that Schumpeter bore anti-Slav prejudices.[22] And indeed, anti-Slav prejudice, along with anti-Semitism, were characteristic elements of Nazi ideology, intersecting in the view that only a purified Germany could save European society from a joint Bolshevik and Jewish threat. Relatively recent evidence points to a strain of anti-Semitism in Schumpeter's thought, as well. The actual substance of his anti-Semitic comments seems rooted less in Nazism itself than in prejudices that were widespread and widely tolerated in central Europe for decades. He made comments and jokes, for example, about Jews' supposed clannishness and their reputed unfair advantages in intellect (Allen 1991, 2: 66–7; Swedberg 1991b, 150). And he was concerned not to be thought of as Jewish (Schumpeter 2000, 243).

Scholars differ on what to make of the signs of these hatreds and sympathies, some taking a sharply critical view, and others putting emphasis on different asserted mitigations and extenuations, from psychological depression to political inexperience, to the fact that pro-Nazi arguments did not generally make their way into his publications.

One possible response to Schumpeter's sympathy for Nazi Germany would be to assume that this sentiment really determined his other political beliefs. This is often our response when we find someone or some group has harbored repugnant opinions. And sometimes it is a quite plausible interpretation. But in Schumpeter's case, such an approach seems wrong. Schumpeter's conservatism had its own logic and its own characteristic premises, distinct from those of Nazi ideology. And as a practical matter, there is a great deal we can learn from analyzing that logic and those premises themselves, even if we disagree. Moreover, it is difficult to imagine that as sophisticated a historian as Schumpeter could have taken seriously certain aspects of Nazi ideology, especially Aryan mythology. But these considerations hardly absolve him. For although his Nazi sympathies probably do not explain Schumpeter's political views in general, the converse is quite plausible. That is, his political commitments do help us account for his sympathy for Nazi Germany. For Schumpeter seems to have thought sympathy for Nazism was natural for a conservative in search of a means of blocking or slowing the pace of deplored change.

When we turn from Schumpeter's relationship to Nazism to his anti-Semitic comments, we find again that interpreters have responded differently to the evidence, with some denying its significance in light of "historical context" (Stolper 1994, 11), others conceding that Schumpeter had "a series of prejudices about the Jews" that caused him sometimes to "vent his personal rage" against them when he was "off balance" (Swedberg 1991b, 150), and others adopting less charitable attitudes (Allen 1991, 2: 66–7; Medearis 2001, 58–73). It is important, of course, to be precise about what is in need of explanation. None of Schumpeter's public writings advance sustained anti-Semitic arguments. And in particular, neither his public nor his private writings articulate substantively the specific ideas and themes that set Nazism apart from other anti-Semitic movements—what Saul Friedländer (1997, 100) calls "redemptive anti-Semitism," the view that the German national struggle against Jews was "metahistorical" and could result only in "perdition or redemption." But although Schumpeter may not have shared in the Nazi ideology of "redemptive anti-Semitism," it would be wrong to suggest that his anti-Semitism had nothing to do Nazism, much less that Nazism caused him to reconsider or soften his anti-Semitism. Schumpeter took part in the efforts to help German Jewish scholars who lost their jobs in Nazi purges, but he also insisted that he was motivated by personal, collegial duty, not by public "protest" against Nazi racial policies (Schumpeter 2000, 243, 253). And it is unquestionably in the historical context of the Nazi rise to power that he wrote in his diary such comments as "We must have either Hitler or else the Jews" and "I am as antisemitic as Schmidt or some kind of rich German-American" (Allen 1991, 2: 66).[23]

The end of the war, though it upset Schumpeter for a time, also reduced the salience of the issues and sympathies that had divided him from those around him. Students flooded back to Harvard, and Schumpeter immersed himself in teaching. His work on the *History of Economic Analysis* continued, as well. But so did his ritual communication with Annie and his mother. Schumpeter's depression persisted as well, now characterized by a growing conviction that he would die soon. It was in fact Elizabeth whose health was in danger first, however. Already living with diabetes, she was diagnosed with breast cancer in the fall of 1948. Schumpeter was stricken with fear, but after radical surgery, she seemed to be out of danger, and the couple returned as best they could to normal life. Indeed, the months following Elizabeth's ordeal were actually productive ones for Schumpeter. Late in 1948, in his presidential address to the American Economic Association, he delivered a speech titled "Science and Ideology," and a version of these remarks became one of six essays he published in 1949, several of which are among his most subtle and interesting, if perhaps not his most influential. In the midst of this professional outpouring, Schumpeter went to bed one evening in January, 1950, apparently reading plays by Euripides in the original Greek until he could sleep.[24] In the middle of the night he had a massive stroke; he died several hours later. He had not quite reached his 67th birthday. But in two-thirds of a century, the provincial boy from Triesch had traveled a very long way, geographically and socially. He had left the town of his ancestors decisively behind and become deeply attached to a form and a strata of society and politics that vanished abruptly when he was still only 35. Then he had continued to move, and continued to think and to write. But he had never found a resting place, personally, intellectually, or politically. Dissatisfaction had come to characterize much of his social thought—and this trait has made recapturing his political and social thought a challenge, as we shall see.

2

Critical Exposition

Tracing Schumpeter's biographical journey has helped us identify the forces that shaped his earliest political perspective. We have seen how broad historical trends interacted with death and ambition to place the son of a provincial manufacturer in surroundings that fostered strong attachments to the Old Regime and to capitalism. But except in probing Schumpeter's "Tory democracy" memos, we have seen little of the substance of his political thought so far. This chapter surveys the Austrian's formidable writings on diverse subjects from entrepreneurship to imperialism, partly for their intrinsic interest, but also with attention to their political content and implications. Although many scholars prefer not to consider Schumpeter political at all, I argue that taken as a whole, his work deserves to be called conservative both because it was broadly oriented toward the prospects for conserving features of existing society, and because it developed a series of classically conservative themes, such as doubts about the capabilities and scope of human rationality. Understanding Schumpeter's conservatism, then, involves first understanding why it is that he thought the form of society he most prized was imperiled. The latter sections of this chapter, accordingly, explore Schumpeter's theory of capitalist crisis, which crucially involves ideas about the decay of old regime institutions and relations.

The earlier sections, to an extent, lay the groundwork for that discussion. In order to understand Schumpeter's theory of the crisis of the capitalist "order," it will be necessary first to understand his theory of the stability of the capitalist "system"—or what we can term "equilibrium economics." In order to understand how Schumpeter eventually came to argue that an equilibrium view of economics could not tell conservatives what they needed to know about imminent social change, we first have to understand his early infatuation with equilibrium models. But the next few sections of this chapter do not merely prepare the way for a later investigation of Schumpeter's political project. For they also shed light on his mature vision of capitalism's process of "creative destruction"—his view of what was most praiseworthy and valuable about capitalism. And there is no doubt that this vision, too, tells us a great deal about Schumpeter's political commitments. Along the way, we will also be able to see some of the features of Schumpeter's economic thought—especially his treatment of the routine conduct of consumers and business people—that contrast with those of other important conservatives whose visions were, like Schumpeter's, rooted in economics. These contrasts will begin to demonstrate not just that Schumpeter was a conservative, but also the kind of rearguard conservative he was.

Equilibrium Economics

A vision of the self-adjusting capitalist economy remained important to Schumpeter throughout his entire career. This is in one sense hardly a surprise, since Schumpeter was both a central figure in the mainstream of twentieth-century economics and a staunch defender of capitalism. But while other stalwarts, such as the economic libertarian Friedrich von Hayek, found in markets an exemplar of spontaneous order, a happy synthesis of freedom and stability, Schumpeter never invested his theoretical conception of self-adjusting market systems with such intrinsic ethical value or indeed any tinge of romance.[1] For one thing, his appreciation of capitalism had a different focus, as we shall see: freewheeling and disruptive innovation. In fact Schumpeter sometimes professed to find the self-adjusting economic actor a bit dull, even contemptible. Even in the work most concerned with economic equilibrium, Schumpeter poked fun at the view of the *homo economicus*—the constantly recalculating consumer or producer of textbook equilibrium economics—as a "miserable figure" lacking "force and life."[2] And although equilibrium was crucially important in Schumpeter's early thought, and always remained a reference point later, it also came to occupy a smaller and smaller part of his thinking. Still, it is necessary to begin with equilibrium to understand the structure of the rest of his thought and even, ultimately, the nature of his conservatism. For conservative arguments did not appear in Schumpeter's writings until the First World War, during which he became convinced both that capitalism was endangered, and that the danger could not be explained in terms of capitalism's self-adjusting, equilibrium properties.

Schumpeter, as we have seen, began studying at the University of Vienna in 1901, just after Carl Menger, one of the founders of neoclassical economics, stopped teaching there. Menger, along with William Stanley Jevons and Léon Walras, had in many people's view revolutionized economics by overturning previous theories of value—theories that attempted to explain the prices for which commodities sell. Earlier, such theories had most often been based on the cost of production, and especially on the amount of labor used to produce goods. Neoclassical theory replaced labor theories with an approach that stressed, in different degrees, an individualist psychology of "utility," the integration of different actors into a view of the whole interrelated economic system, and the possibility of mathematizing economics. Menger's part in this emphasized the principle of declining "marginal utility," the idea that a consumer's desire for an additional portion of any good necessarily declines as she obtains successive increments of it. While Menger insisted that this was a psychological fact, Walras was more interested in the way that the concept of declining marginal utility, or its mathematical expression, made it possible to model an entire interconnected economy of utility-maximizing consumers and producers.

The Nature and Essence of Theoretical Economics, Schumpeter's 1908 *Habilitationsschrift*, was largely a survey and tribute to Walras's approach. For Schumpeter, the crux of the neoclassical economics of Menger, Walras, and Jevons was equilibrium itself. It constituted the foundation of the discipline. Equilibrium models, as Schumpeter understood them, consisted of behavior rules that economic actors were assumed to follow—most generally, the assumption that actors attempted to maximize their own utility—along with "functional" or algebraically expressed relationships among such actors and the various "economic quantities" in the system—for example, equations showing how demand for a good may vary with its price (Schumpeter 1908, 28). Equilibrium models also were based on the assumption of mutual dependence, in so far as a change in any quantity in the system would ultimately result in an adjustment in all of them. And finally, as the name indicates, such models assumed that the system would have a tendency to move toward a balance between forces, to stabilize itself after a change. The idea that the components of such a system were, on the one hand, measurable economic "quantities" and, on the other, relations among those quantities expressed as algebraic functions, underscored for Schumpeter that the mathematizing of economics was crucial. Indeed, following Walras, Schumpeter thought an equilibrium model could be summarized as a set of simultaneous algebraic equations. And this meant that in principle, it would be possible to find a set of values defining a mathematical solution—in practical terms, a set of prices at which markets would clear and every actor's utility would be maximized.

This, as I have indicated, was a decidedly Walrasian view of the new economics. Appropriately enough, then, Schumpeter wrote to Walras in Lausanne after the publication of *Theoretical Economics* in 1908, promising to send a copy, and calling himself a "disciple" and his book an "homage" (Schumpeter 2000, 43). Perhaps for this reason, when Menger's student and successor at the University of Vienna, Friedrich von Wieser, reviewed the book, he chastised Schumpeter—in particular, for rejecting a direct role for psychology in economics (Allen 1991, 1: 83). For

Schumpeter had argued that economists could be indifferent to the question whether it was psychologically realistic to assume economic actors rationally calculated the "marginal utility" of different choices available to them. The concept was useful economically only for the fully developed model of the economy that could be based upon it. Many years after publishing *Theoretical Economics*, Schumpeter would write:

> So soon as we realize that it is the general-equilibrium system which is the really important thing, we discover that, in itself, the principle of marginal utility is not so important after all as Jevons, the Austrians, and Walras himself believed. But analysis of Walras's schema at the time discloses the fact that marginal utility was the ladder by which Walras climbed to the level of his general-equilibrium system. If the marginal utility principle ceased to be all-important after this level had been reached, it was nevertheless all-important heuristically. (Schumpeter [1954] 1994, 918)

Schumpeter's relative indifference to the theory of marginal utility as a psychology of human needs is interesting for two further reasons for students of social and political theory. First it is related to his coining of the expression, "methodological individualism" (Schumpeter 1908, 88). The theory of marginal utility was both subjective and individualist in outlook, insisting that the economy was simply a system of prices derived from the subjective value that individuals themselves placed on goods, rather than from any intrinsic qualities of the goods themselves.[3] We have already seen that Schumpeter was mainly interested in this assumption as a "ladder" upon which economic theorists could climb, declining to vouch for its usefulness outside pure economics. Similarly, but more broadly, he insisted that the adoption of an individualist viewpoint as a matter of economic methodology did not imply or require an individualist viewpoint in political matters. He argued: "[T]here exists not the slightest connection between individualistic science and political individualism" (90). This insistence on sharply distinguishing the assumptions of economic theory from sociological, psychological, or ethical critique also suggested that Schumpeter's conservatism could not draw on individualist economic assumptions, as others' so often have. Here it is useful again to draw a contrast with Hayek, who drew broadly political conclusions from what he took to be a basic fact about the capitalist economy: that it allowed individuals to choose and to act freely according to the values that they themselves placed on goods (Hayek [1944] 1994, 41–2). And the contrast between Schumpeter and Hayek is not due only to Schumpeter's insistence on separating economic science from politics, but also to the fact that Schumpeter simply never believed, as Hayek did, that consumers chose freely in any meaningful sense. In the 1940s, he would insist that consumer choices were manipulated by entrepreneurs—not products of genuine free choice at all. Consumers, he wrote, "are so amenable to the influence of advertising and other methods of persuasion that producers often seem to dictate to them instead of being directed by them" (Schumpeter [1942] 1976, 257). And as early as 1911, Schumpeter insisted that entrepreneurs had to teach consumers to want new products—rather than wait for consumers to decide, rationally, that they needed or wanted them (Schumpeter [1911] 1934, 10).

Schumpeter laid out his equilibrium vision in his *Habilitationsschrift* and returned to it in essentially every important work thereafter. In his *Theory of Economic Development* (*Theorie der Wirtschaftlichen Entwicklung*, 1911) and a few years later, in *Economic Doctrine and Method* (*Epochen der Dogmen- und Methodengeschichte*, 1914), it was the "circular flow of economic life," a vision of an economy humming along, producing the same things in the same way, without (for reasons we shall soon see) the interventions of entrepreneurs (Schumpeter, [1911] 1934, ch. 1). In *Business Cycles*, it reappeared as the "businessman's normal" and the "stationary flow," both referring to a "model of an unchanging economic process which flows on at constant rates in time and merely reproduces itself" (Schumpeter 1939, 3, 35–6). In *Capitalism, Socialism and Democracy* a trace of this vision is found in Schumpeter's mention of "equilibrium, i.e., a determinate state of the economic organism, toward which any given state of it is always gravitating and which displays certain simple properties" (Schumpeter [1942] 1976, 79).

Yet even early on, it is clear that Schumpeter thought equilibrium models, valuable though they were, were only a small part of economic science—and that equilibrium tendencies were only one feature of capitalism. What would change over time for him is how he would understand and evaluate this judgment. In *Theoretical Economics*, Schumpeter insisted almost fiercely that equilibrium models were a small but absolutely sovereign kingdom, separate from practical affairs, studies of economic dynamics, from historical investigation of how the economy got to be the way it is and from the fields of sociology, metaphysics, ethics, and philosophy (Schumpeter 1908, xix, 52, 93, 536). In just a few years, however, he would write that "the social process is really one indivisible whole," suggesting that one could be at best provisionally satisfied with the findings of equilibrium models (Schumpeter [1911] 1934, 3). And late in his career, he would insist that of all the "fundamental fields" of economics, "economic history"—not economic "theory," with its equilibrium models—was "by far the most important" (Schumpeter [1954] 1994, 12).

Innovation and Creative Destruction

Although Schumpeter merely sent a copy of *Theoretical Economics* to Walras in the year of its publication, he did finally make the trip to Lausanne to visit Walras himself the following year. As Schumpeter told the story many decades later, his developing attitude toward Walras's achievements was underscored by an exchange that took place during this meeting. After *Theoretical Economics*, Schumpeter was attempting to construct a theory of economic development, a theory of how the economic system itself generated (and did not merely respond to) change. And he had come to the conclusion that Walras's economic model was not only "static" in character but was also capable of explaining only a "stationary" economy (Schumpeter [1937] 1989, 165). This distinction in terms is a difficult one. The adjective "static," as Schumpeter used it, applies to the models economists use to depict and study the economy, whereas "stationary" refers to actual economies themselves. So Schumpeter's point was that it was widely understood that Walras's model could be used only to demonstrate how the economy would adjust to external disturbances, such as "natural catastrophes, wars and so on" (166). It was less obvious, he thought, but true, that Walras also assumed that the economy really was "stationary" that it "does not change of its own initiative, but merely reproduces constant rates of real income as it flows along in time" (166).

This was the nub and essence of Schumpeter's growing dissatisfaction with Walras's work, and his later narrative suggests that Schumpeter quizzed the aging French economist about it. Schumpeter would later write that "Walras would have admitted" viewing the capitalist economy as stationary:

> He would have said (and, as a matter of fact, he did say it to me the only time that I had the opportunity to converse with him) that of course economic life is essentially passive and merely adapts itself to the natural and social influences which may be acting on it, so that the theory of a stationary process constitutes really the whole of theoretical economics and that as economic theorists we cannot say much about the factors that account for historical change, but must simply register them. Like the classics, he would have made exceptions for increase in population and in savings, but this would only introduce a change in the data of the system and not add any new phenomena. I felt very strongly that this was wrong, and that there was a source of energy within the economic system which would of itself disrupt any equilibrium that might be attained. (Schumpeter [1937] 1989, 166)

This is no mere quibble, but the origin of Schumpeter's distinctive contribution to economics, one still celebrated by both scholars and journalists: his interrelated theories of the entrepreneur, innovation, and "creative destruction."

These theories can initially be grasped in a contrast between ordinary economic conduct and the action of a few individuals: entrepreneurs.[4] According to the pure economic theory of Schumpeter's youth, equilibrium was seen as resulting from constant, almost seamless rational calculation by consumers and producers seeking their own highest good or utility. Schumpeter believed that this assumption of rational utility calculation was extremely useful in that it allowed the field of economics to attain a kind of semiautonomy from sociology, history, and political science. That is, it gave economists a bold and autonomous foundational assumption for studying the properties of capitalist markets without being encumbered by muddying details about the actual cultural and social practices of different capitalist societies. But, simply put, he thought the assumption was also very often untrue. In reality, the capitalist system showed a tendency toward equilibrium, a tendency to reach a balance after disturbances, not because actors smoothly updated their rational utility calculations, but because they followed traditional and customary procedures (Schumpeter [1911] 1934, 42). Schumpeter would later write that "this is the only way in which the majority of people do act and are capable of acting" (Schumpeter [1927] 1989, 27).

Certain economic actors, however, were able at times to break from custom or tradition. These actors, when they took on the role of "entrepreneurs" rather than "mere managers," devised innovations: new products, new ways of making products, and even new ways of delivering products. Schumpeter was always keen to stress that innovation was not to be confused with invention or discovery (Schumpeter [1927] 1989, 28). A scientist might discover a material, or an inventor lay the groundwork for a new technology without having the social and institutional skill or the personal drive to actually bring it to market. Furthermore, social life presented many forms of resistance to the new, which those wishing to introduce innovations had to overcome. Because both the easy availability of inventions and social resistance to their application could be taken as constants, Schumpeter argued that it was "more by will than by intellect" that entrepreneurs carried out their innovating role (Schumpeter [1911] 1934, 88). Entrepreneurs were the characteristic (but not the only) leaders of capitalist society—as important and distinctive as feudal warriors in another era.

Entrepreneurial innovation was, in Schumpeter's vision, the engine that actually propelled economic development. And just as innovation was distinct from the sort of conduct that constituted day-to-day economic life, such development was quite different from what equilibrium economics might lead one to expect. Not to be measured simply in growing national production, higher incomes, or a burgeoning population, economic development in Schumpeter's sense of the term was:

> a distinct phenomenon, entirely foreign to what may be observed in the circular flow or in the tendency towards equilibrium. It is spontaneous and discontinuous change in the channels of the flow, disturbance of equilibrium, which forever alters and displaces the equilibrium state previously existing. (Schumpeter [1911] 1934, 64)

While building a railroad in the nineteenth century might be an example of internally driven economic development, as Schumpeter understood it, simply adding another stagecoach to an existing fleet was an example of ordinary equilibrating adjustment to such external changes as population growth (Schumpeter [1911] 1934, 62, 66). More specifically, innovation, according to Schumpeter, could take five forms: new products, new methods of production, the opening of new markets, the "conquest" of new sources of materials, and the institutional reorganization of a business institution (66).

Because from our later standpoint it seems so clear that Schumpeter was breaking with the form of economics focused on the study and manipulation of equilibrium models, the subtle influences of Walrasian economics on him may not be very clear. But recognizing a few of these influences can help clarify Schumpeter's particular contribution for us. Schumpeter, like Walras, saw production primarily as the *combination* of factors of production according to certain proportions. The key role of the Schumpeterian entrepreneur, viewed in these terms, was that he or she changed the recipe—introduced "*new combinations*" of factors.

Yet while the entrepreneur's economic activity could be described in terms of such new contributions and their reverberating effects on the economy, Schumpeter was insistent that the motivation for such innovation could, again, not be grasped from the standpoint of ordinary neoclassical economics. Such economics, founded on the idea of marginal utility, made the satisfaction of wants and needs both the "meaning" and the "motive" of economic activity (Schumpeter [1911] 1934, 91). But Schumpeter argued that an entrepreneur did not innovate in order to satisfy her own or others' wants, or even to maximize her own income from profits. Why then expend the effort to overcome such entrenched social resistance to change? "First of all," wrote Schumpeter:

> there is the dream and the will to found a private kingdom, usually, though not necessarily, also a dynasty. The modern world really does not know any such positions, but what may be attained by industrial or commercial success is still the nearest approach to medieval lordship possible to modern man . . . Then there is the will to conquer; the impulse to fight, to prove oneself superior to others, to succeed for the sake, not of the fruits of success, but of success itself. From this aspect, economic action becomes akin to sport—there are financial races, or rather boxing matches . . . Finally, there is the joy of creating, of getting things done, or simply of exercising one's energy and ingenuity. (93)

Although in a book focused on his political thought, a full exposition of Schumpeter's model of economic development is unnecessary, it is worthwhile for even the general-interest reader to understand how far-reaching were the implications of Schumpeter's view of innovation and nonequilibrium economics, the extent to which they implied different, sometimes novel approaches to a diverse set of standard topics in economics. We can begin to do this by reference to textbook neoclassical economic theory, which in its most abstract form would suggest that in a fully competitive equilibrating market, contending producers would drive prices down to the point where profits would disappear, an axiom Schumpeter accepted (Schumpeter [1911] 1934, 46, 129). But essentially by stressing this axiom very strongly, Schumpeter argued that equilibrium approaches, on their own, could not explain the existence of profits—nor of credit, interest, or capital, as he understood them. At the same time Schumpeter insisted for similar reasons that under equilibrium circumstances there could never be idle productive resources—resources available, most importantly, to be combined in new ways to create innovative products and services. For axiomatically, under competitive circumstances, idle resources would simply fall in price until purchased and used. The key point in this, for Schumpeter, was that entrepreneurs, unlike ordinary producers, could earn profits, because for a time they produced and sold their products without direct competitors putting pressure on prices (130–1). With the promise of future profits, he reasoned, would-be entrepreneurs could promise to pay interest on bank loans, and those loans could be used to purchase resources that were otherwise committed to existing production, and to redirect them to innovative productive uses (157–8). On the other hand, in the absence of entrepreneurial profits, he insisted, such interest could not exist, nor could capital, understood simply as purchasing power available to entrepreneurs (116).

According to Schumpeter's vision, innovation could also explain the capitalist economy's alternating periods of expansion and recession. Although he broached the subject in *Theory of Economic Development*, he developed it far more thoroughly in *Business Cycles* (1939), a book he regarded as being built with help from the "scaffolding" of the earlier exploration (Schumpeter

1939, v). The first chapters of *Business Cycles* recapitulated and expanded upon many arguments Schumpeter introduced decades earlier in *Economic Development.* Innovation or entrepreneurial activity could be understood as qualitatively different from the forms of conduct that were at the center of equilibrium models. "Everyone knows," he wrote, "that to do something new is very much more difficult than to do something that belongs to the realm of routine, and that the two tasks differ qualitatively and not only in degree" (99). Such things as changes in consumer tastes, population growth, and even savings could not adequately account for capitalist dynamism, he contended (73, 74, 76). What mattered was innovation, the creation of new commodities, new productive methods, and new business institutions. In comparison to innovation, mere invention was "without importance to economic analysis" (85). But innovation, by contrast, was what explained why "the history of capitalism is studded with violent bursts and catastrophes . . . more like a series of explosions than a gentle, though incessant, transformation" (102).

The remainder of the book, then, went well beyond *Economic Development*'s attempts to explain economic cycles, elaborating on the phenomena involved, and using extensive historical data to map out what he thought was a reasoned history of the capitalist process. The explanation begins with claims about the pace and timing of innovation. For Schumpeter contended that innovations did not appear in a steady stream. As he put it in *Economic Development*: "new combinations are not, as one would expect according to general principles of probability, evenly distributed through time . . . but appear, if at all, discontinuously, in groups or swarms" (Schumpeter [1911] 1934, 223). An initial innovation by one business then made possible an expanding wave of imitation, bringing the innovation to a new range of applications. Schumpeter believed that the initial innovation required unusual leadership ability, but that the spread and continued application of the innovation throughout an economy required less and less ability, because those who went first showed the way to the others.

But why should these bursts of innovation have caused cycles of boom and bust, leading such things as borrowing, interest rates, aggregate production, aggregate consumption and wages to rise and fall cyclically over time? And why, when they fell, should they fall so far and so precipitously as to cause a recession? It is perhaps easiest to understand Schumpeter's argument if we begin with the factors contributing to the cyclical rise of these measures—and more particularly, with borrowing.[5] Schumpeter's view, remember, was that in an equilibrium economy, production would be financed by regular business receipts, and no resources would be available for new kinds of production. To overcome this situation, the entrepreneur essentially had to borrow from a bank, which could in effect create money for the purpose by means of the fractional reserve system (the system by which banks keep in reserve some, but not all, the money they receive from depositors). The entrepreneur's borrowing (later augmented by that of imitators) tended at the outset of the cycle to drive up interest rates. Of course, the entrepreneur, in Schumpeter's view, would next use the loan to purchase materials and hire workers, and create new products, thus tending to drive up commodity prices and wages and increase aggregate production. Assuming the innovation was a genuine one, it would presumably allow the new business to earn a profit, essentially because its cost of production would be well below that of competitors. The same would be true for some of those following in the leader's footsteps. The resulting profits and the higher wages and prices would eventually proliferate through the entire economy. A favorite example for Schumpeter was Richard Arkwright's early harnessing of water power for textile production, which allowed his factory to undersell those still producing on hand looms (and helped launch the industrial revolution). All these factors contributed to the upward sweep of the business cycle.

As for the downward portion of the cycle, the new businesses would put in peril many older ones using older methods—and many would fail. Moreover, miscalculation played an important role in Schumpeter's model. He argued that in addition to innovators, others in the same line of business would also borrow in order to expand production, leading to the same kind of effects on interest rates, prices, and wages. But these ventures were sometimes ill-conceived, and for this reason, the boom phase of the business cycle would overshoot its mark. Eventually all those loans would have to be repaid, decreasing borrowing and interest rates. Moreover, failing businesses would tend to contribute to declining interest rates, prices, and wages.

At the time that he wrote the earlier book, Schumpeter believed there was essentially one kind of wavelike economic motion caused by innovations and their spread through the economy. By the time that he wrote *Business Cycles*, he had decided one could discern three types, superimposed on each other, each of a different duration (or one might say, wavelength), and each named for a different economist who had developed a cyclical theory around the wave. In addition to the "Juglar" cycles of about a decade, there were 40-month "Kitchin" cycles, and 40–50 year "Kondratieff" cycles.[6]

It is important to note that from the outset many economists have been dissatisfied with the explanation of cycles just elaborated. In particular, for example, they have asked why Schumpeter should have assumed that innovations appeared in clusters, with lulls in between (Kuznets 1940, 262; Lange 1941, 1902; Marschak 1940, 892). Why should we not assume that innovations occur evenly and regularly (or better yet, randomly) so that the "cyclical" effects of different randomly occurring innovations would essentially cancel each other out? Others have focused their skepticism on Schumpeter's derivation of so many different cycles from a single phenomenon, innovation. Defenders have not so much claimed that Schumpeter was right about these matters as they have pointed out that both *Economic Development* and *Business Cycles* are rich and full of insight—economic, methodological, and sociological.

In any case, of the three waves Schumpeter described, it is really the Kondratieff that provides the basic periodic structure to the historical and statistical discussion that forms so much of *Business Cycles*, making it a history of capitalism as much as a work of economic theory. According to Schumpeter, by 1939, capitalism (essentially in Germany, the United Kingdom and the United States) had been through three major innovation-driven cycles. The first of these, from 1786 to 1842, began with the industrial revolution, and was driven by innovations in water and steam power. The second, from 1843 to 1897, Schumpeter sometimes termed the "bourgeois" Kondratieff (Schumpeter 1939, 305). In his view, this cycle was spurred more than anything else by the building of railroads. The third Kondratieff, dated from 1898 to his publication date in 1939, Schumpeter termed the "New Industrial Revolution," although it also contained within it the years of the Great Depression. Schumpeter linked this cycle most of all to electricity, but also to the automobile and innovations in chemicals. One can easily see here the master narrative: each of these longest cycles was associated not so much with a single product or process innovation but massive changes such as electrification that were really bundles of innovations, working their way through the economy over very long periods of time, almost lifetimes.

The framework of Schumpeter's theory of the "capitalist process" was fully worked out in *Business Cycles* and did not change in its fundamentals in *Capitalism, Socialism and Democracy* (1942), though a term he coined for that volume is the one most readers probably associate with Schumpeter's approach: "the process of creative destruction." The compact section that begins the chapter by that title serves as a summary of Schumpeter's approach and its political significance. The immediate purpose of the chapter was to rebut the claim that the growth of large corporations with monopolistic market power, though created by capitalism, would be its undoing. Although it would take more space than is justified here to explain Schumpeter's views of imperfect competition, it should be clear enough from the foregoing that he did not think that capitalism's value or its driving force was derived from perfect competition and the related tendency of competition to return the economy to an equilibrium state. Far from it. In fact, Schumpeter had much to say in appreciation of monopolistic corporations and their ability to sustain innovation and increase the standard of living. Surveying the historical record, he claimed, "a shocking suspicion dawns upon us that big business may have had more to do with creating that standard of life than with keeping it down" (Schumpeter [1942] 1976, 82). It is in this connection that he continued, criticizing the competition-and-equilibrium-centered view of capitalism, and providing this perfect distillation of his thought:

> Capitalism, then, is by nature a form or method of economic change and not only never is but never can be stationary. And this evolutionary character of the capitalist process is not merely due to the fact that economic life goes on in a social and natural environment which changes and by its change alters the data of economic action . . . Nor is this evolutionary character due to a quasi-automatic increase in population and capital or to the vagaries of monetary systems . . . The fundamental impulse that sets and keeps the capitalist engine in motion comes from the new consumers' goods, the new methods of production or transportation, the new markets, the new forms of industrial organization that capitalist enterprise creates . . . [T]he history of the productive apparatus of a typical farm, from the beginnings of the rationalization of crop rotation, plowing and fattening to the mechanized thing of today—linking up with elevators and railroads—is a history of revolutions. So is the history of the productive apparatus of the iron and steel industry from the charcoal furnace to our own type of furnace, or the history of power production from the overshot water wheel to the modern power plant, or the history of transportation from the mail-coach to the airplane. The opening of new markets, foreign or domestic, and the organizational development from the craft shop and factory to such concerns as U.S. Steel illustrate the same process of industrial mutation—if I may use that biological term—that

incessantly revolutionizes the economic structure *from within*, incessantly destroying the old one, incessantly creating a new one. This process of Creative Destruction is the essential fact about capitalism. (Schumpeter [1942] 1976, 82–3)

This fine summary of Schumpeter's vision points to some distinctive political or policy implications. Now, Schumpeter would have insisted that *Economic Development* and *Business Cycles*, in particular, were not political books, and he scorned those who in his view shortchanged intellectual rigor for quick policy prescriptions. But Schumpeter's economic theory and vision were part of a comprehensive view that had strongly political elements, and in works like *Capitalism, Socialism and Democracy*, these implications were more visible, though they were by no means fully hidden elsewhere. Schumpeter was always an ardent supporter of capitalism, but unlike those who see its essence as open competition enabled by widespread personal freedom, Schumpeter was compelled more by capitalism's destructive, unpredictable side, and the opening for expression it gave to a small and distinct group of people with great leadership ability. For Schumpeter, innovation and entrepreneurship were not only not identical with competitive equilibrium, as it is normally understood—they disrupted it. And there was in Schumpeter's writings little emphasis on the claim that capitalism entails economic freedom or room for initiative for the average person. He criticized Hayek for forgetting that "individual initiative and self-reliance are the principles of a very limited class. They mean nothing to the mass of people who—no matter for what reason—are not up to the standard they imply" (Schumpeter 1946, 270). Nor was he inclined to claim that capitalism, of its own, was a tranquil system, more likely to fulfill than to upset anyone's life plans, and only itself disturbed by external shocks like wars and droughts. Schumpeter insisted that a crucial cause of depressions was to be found in capitalism itself. And indeed that cause was co-original with capitalism's energy. Furthermore, he asked that, like him, readers embrace or at least accept that destruction.

Approaching the matter from another direction—and pointing to another important contrast—we might notice Schumpeter was not alone in seeing economic downturns as arising from capitalism's own fundamental workings. So too did John Maynard Keynes and, indeed, so did Karl Marx. But Schumpeter's vision of capitalism distinguished him just as much from their economics and politics. For while he saw in capitalism the mechanism for depressions, he insisted that capitalism was not prone to crises, in the sense of irresolvable, self-generated breakdowns. Capitalism did not need to be saved from itself, as Keynes might have thought, nor could it be hurried along toward its own self-inflicted mortality—if that death were seen as due to purely "economic" causes. As we shall see, however, that was a big "if" in Schumpeter's view. Indeed it is the very subject of capitalism's mortality that gains us the next insight into Schumpeter's politics.

The Capitalist Order: The Tax State, Imperialism, and Social Classes

So far, I have traced Schumpeter's theory of innovation from its origins in his thought around 1910 to its fullest statement in the 1940s as part of a history of capitalism. While this idea is perhaps Schumpeter's most widely noted contribution to economics, and its elucidation shows us what Schumpeter admired in capitalism, the discussion so far has only begun to shed light on his political ideas. For Schumpeter is best understood not only in light of what he wished to preserve but also what he thought threatened it.

Indeed, until the trauma of the First World War, Schumpeter may not have been particularly conscious of himself as a conservative. That is, although he must surely have had affinities for what he would soon call the conservative "circles" and for traditional Austro-Hungarian society and politics, the purpose of preserving aspects of the world he loved had probably not yet consciously guided to his writings. The war, it seems likely, forced Schumpeter, along with many others, to confront the question whether capitalism—and more especially, the whole society in which the capitalism of his time was embedded—could survive. There is evidence for this both in the fact that he wrote on certain topics at this time, as well as in the writings themselves. His 1918 essay on the "Tax State," for example, was motivated by precisely the urge to answer this question, even though now some may read it simply as a contribution to fiscal policy analysis. As Schumpeter put it there: "Many people assert, and indeed in some circles it has become axiomatic, that the fiscal problems left in the wake of the war cannot be solved within the framework of our prewar economic order" (Schumpeter [1918] 1991, 99). By this time, Schumpeter had already written his conservative "Tory democracy" memos, which I discussed in the previous chapter. And within a few years after the war, he had published the first writings that dealt with his core conservative concern—the fate of capitalism, as he understood it—and elaborated on themes that clearly mark him as a member of the family of conservatives.

Schumpeter's conservative political thought mapped onto the broad view of social science—or of the relation of different social science topics to each other—that he had already been developing prior to the war. He had argued, as we have seen, for the relative autonomy of pure economics from sociology, psychology, and political science—in fact, for the existence of purely economic forces and mechanisms, such as equilibrium and innovation, distinct from noneconomic matters, such as wars or cultural changes affecting consumer tastes. This is significant because it is fairly clear, as we have seen, that while Schumpeter thought the capitalist economy or system, as driven forward by innovation, was changeable and tumultuous, it was also stable, in the sense that it did not tend to produce forces necessitating its own demise.

But at some point between the publication of *Economic Development* in 1911 and "The Crisis of the Tax State" in 1918 it seems to have struck him forcefully—although how suddenly, it is impossible to say—that in itself this view was inadequate to determining the future of capitalism. It was, as he would write a decade later, "no more sufficient as a basis for prediction than a doctor's diagnosis to the effect that a man has no cancer is a sufficient basis for the prediction that he will go on living indefinitely" (Schumpeter [1928] 1989, 71). This will be our bridge to a new set of topics.

To introduce some useful terminology, Schumpeter had come to think that the theory of economic development was sufficient to establish the stability of the "capitalist system." But it could say nothing about the stability of the "capitalist order." For Schumpeter, the capitalist "system" meant just the economy, a network of "independent quantities"—things such as prices and incomes—all "mutually determining each other" (Schumpeter [1928] 1989, 50). The capitalist "order" referred to a whole set of surrounding institutions, beliefs, and practices, necessary for the functioning of the system (49). While *Theoretical Economics* and *Economic Development* focused almost exclusively on the capitalist "system," Schumpeter's writings on the history and future development of capitalist societies—the writings most proximate to his conservative concerns—would hereafter emphasize or at least include analyses of the capitalist "order."

In the next sections, then, I explore three of Schumpeter's most famous essays on "economic sociology," which for now we may understand as the study of the institutions and practices of the capitalist "order" most relevant to the survival of the capitalist "system." These are "The Crisis of the Tax State," published in 1918, "The Sociology of Imperialisms," published in 1918–19, and "Social Classes in an Ethnically Homogenous Environment" published in 1927. These essays are both remarkably diverse and yet interconnected. And each is known for offering a distinctive answer to a classic sociological problem or controversy.

The Tax State

To write about the "tax state" was for Schumpeter to write about the capitalist order *and* the capitalist system, jointly, and from a particular point of view. We could call that vantage point "fiscal sociology," but Schumpeter was up to something a bit more than just a sociological examination of the sources of state revenue. He set out to analyze the capitalist economy and the capitalist state, the capitalist system and the surrounding capitalist order, in their mutual relation. He wanted as well to understand current economic and fiscal problems in terms of long historical developments shaping them, rather than just the present array of forces.

The culmination of Schumpeter's argument was that "*there is no 'crisis of the tax state'*"—none, that is, at the time of his writing, just at war's end (Schumpeter [1918] 1991, 130). But while, as we have seen, Schumpeter thought that the pure capitalist system was not essentially vulnerable to internally generated crisis, the tax state in principle was vulnerable, even if it did not face immediate crisis. Thus Schumpeter actually ended "Crisis" with a sort of codicil to the effect that "society is growing beyond private enterprise and tax state, not because but in spite of the war" (131). So what would constitute a "crisis?" And what sort of thing *was* the "tax state" that it was not facing crisis, despite the wrenching upheaval caused by the war? The first question is relatively easily answered. A crisis, for Schumpeter, meant "obvious, ineluctable, continuous failure due to unalterable social change" (131). The rest, however, requires more explanation.

One difficulty for contemporary readers is that in this 1918 essay, Schumpeter highlighted and gave a name to something many people now take for granted: a governing entity that was intended, at least, to look after the public good, and which at the same time derived the funds to do so from taxes on private economic activity—activity that was assumed, by contrast, to be pursued for personal, not common and social, ends. As Schumpeter put it, it was "part of its nature" that the state "opposes individual egoism as a representative of the common purpose" (Schumpeter [1918] 1991, 110). He insisted that such an entity as the tax state had not always existed, that the "organizational forms" of the feudal world "combined both what we nowadays call the public and the private sphere in one essentially different unity" (104).[7] The breaking up of this unity and the initial development of the tax state had occurred in response to particular historical strains—more pointedly, a crisis—many centuries before the First World War. Schumpeter argued that the Germanic princes of the sixteenth century faced the need to raise vast mercenary armies to combat the Ottomans—but had only insufficient, feudal revenues to do it. This he termed a "textbook" crisis (106). In order to solve the problem, the princes themselves had to challenge the feudal order. The absence of a clear distinction between public and private realms in feudal life meant that there was no true public political authority, nor any truly private conduct separate from it. A feudal prince looked upon political power "as a *patrimonium* of which he could dispose in a manner which was nobody else's business" (103). And feudal princes, like lesser feudal nobility below them, had direct control of productive resources—they owned, variously, croplands, pastures, and vineyards, as well as exclusive rights to press grapes, grind flour, and receive payments from peasants or serfs both in specie and in labor—so that such military and judicial activities as they undertook did not have to be funded by broad-based taxes. At the same time, of course, it was of the essence of feudal relations that such a prince could call upon on the military service of lesser nobles and knights below him.

But this feudal position was not one from which a prince could raise the huge revenues needed to wage war in an age in growing mercenary armies. Thus such princes[8] devised a novel stratagem. They argued to the feudal estates below them that war-making was a common interest to which they should all contribute revenues. This meant that princes would receive tax revenue from economic activity that was not their own and other members of the nobility would have, in turn, to set aside some of the proceeds of their own economic activity to send to the prince. Where the princes succeeded at this gambit, they initiated the formation of tax states, in Schumpeter's phrase, states existing as powers distinct from a realm of private economic activity, but states that nevertheless both shaped and made important claims against that activity.

Schumpeter insisted that we cannot just see the tax state as a distinct, autonomous entity and the economy as another; each was what it was in part because of its historical relationship to the other. This should be clear from the fact that Schumpeter argued the tax state arose from a particular and new parceling of the social world, a kind of separation that had not existed before. But the relational, codetermining nature of state and economy becomes even clearer when we take into account Schumpeter's insistence that the tax state, through its demands for revenue, essentially reshaped and rationalized economic activity, almost *creating* the truly private economy. That is, the fact of tax collectors constantly hunting down different forms of economic activity and subjecting them to taxation fostered among taxpaying traders and producers a new self-regarding, measuring, calculating spirit.

Over time, in his view, this development had a profoundly corrosive effect on the feudal spirit, which in combining self-interested and communal motivations, had inhibited the pure development of either. It was particularly destructive for the nobility, who began, in a process Schumpeter termed "patrimonialization," to think of their lands as economic assets to be exploited purely for private interest, rather than fiefs for the support of a unique military calling (Schumpeter [1918] 1991, 106). As he put it:

> When the stream of productive revolutions sweeps away this world, when the knight forgets the Holy Grail and bethinks himself of his property, then this order breaks up like a corpse swollen with putrefying gases—and it breaks up into individuals and families with a thousand conflicting interests. (109)

According to Schumpeter, the effect of these related political-economic developments was that that the tax state, after virtually creating the private economy, became dependent upon it. So instead of characterizing the tax state as artificial and antithetical to natural, private economic activity, as some proponents of private enterprise might, Schumpeter emphasized that the tax state had a structurally reinforced reciprocal interest in not doing anything that might jeopardize the health of its income source. He reviewed a wide array of tax types, and indicated how far each could be extended. Although the answer varied from tax to tax, the message was consistent:

> [T]he tax state must not demand from the people so much that they lose financial interest in production or at any rate cease to use their best energies for it. (Schumpeter [1918] 1991, 112)

Some scholars have pointed out here an observation similar to one made popular by the economist Arthur Laffer in the 1970s and 1980s: that beyond a certain point, increases in the rate of taxation should lead to decreases in total tax revenue (Schumpeter [1918] 1991, 113). In a sense, these scholars are right about the similarity. But Schumpeter's purpose was not to argue, as Laffer's adherents in the Reagan administration did, for tax cuts that could lead, according to the argument, to higher state revenues. Rather, Schumpeter sought to define and highlight the nature of a crisis for the tax state: a situation in which the demand for state revenue became so high that it would crush private economic activity upon which the state reciprocally depended. And his point was that such an end for the tax state could only coincide with the end of the capitalist economy, and indeed the whole society built upon a reciprocal relationship between them. When the demands of taxation, the demands of public on private activity, became too great, he wrote: "Then the tax state will have run its course and society will have to depend on other motive forces for its economy than self-interest" (116).

The penultimate portion of the essay was devoted, essentially, to a bit of policy analysis. Interestingly, given the aforementioned analysis of the limits beyond which taxation must not be pushed, Schumpeter argued in favor a type of tax that many conservatives and proponents of free enterprise today would regard as confiscatory: a capital levy (Schumpeter [1918] 1991, 118–26). Briefly,

Schumpeter's point was that after the war, the biggest problem for Austria-Hungary would be war debt—or more particularly, the fact that the state (and to an extent, private entities) had borrowed to purchase things, such as productive resources or war materiel, that had been destroyed by war. In effect, this put the state, particularly, in something like the position of a person whose loan-financed car had been wrecked, or whose mortgage-financed house had burned down. It also created inflationary pressures. He thus suggested, in effect, a "large-scale writing-down of book values," and suggested that this be accomplished with a capital levy, a one time in-kind assessment of credit instruments, especially government war bonds and bank loans. After collecting these instruments from those citizens who held them, the government would essentially destroy them, thereby abolishing a portion of its own debt. Similar proposals for levying financial instruments were advanced by others, including socialists, at the time, but Schumpeter was clear about the contrasting scope and purpose of his proposal. His levy would be onetime only; it would not be used to collect money for government expenditures; and it would not be used for the government to obtain equity interests in private manufacturers.

In light of Schumpeter's conviction that the capitalist system would not on its own collapse, and that a crisis of the tax state was not imminent in 1918, it might seem that he must have been optimistic about capitalism's future. But even in 1918, he was not. His comments on the subject in "Crisis of the Tax State" were terse. But they are unmistakable in their thrust. Society was "growing beyond private enterprise and tax state, not because but in spite of the war" (Schumpeter [1918] 1991, 131). This he attributed, somewhat cryptically, to "private enterprise" losing "its social meaning through the development of the economy and the consequent expansion of the sphere of social sympathy" (131). Although he did not explain himself fully in "Crisis" itself, the culprit seems to have been rationalization, and more specifically, a process of rationalization that enabled innovation to take place without entrepreneurs. This is a crucial claim, and one to which I shall return.

Imperialism

In comparison to the now-forgotten discourse about the possibility that the First World War would foster socialism, the century-old debate about imperialism is generally more familiar to present-day readers, possibly because the participants included such figures as V. I. Lenin. In a sense, this relative familiarity makes it easier to understand part of the apparent purpose behind Schumpeter's intervention—perhaps, even, too easy. One of the main points I want to make about the essay is that it is considerably more complex—even equivocal—than many interpreters have thought.

The subject of imperialism was an important and fiercely contested one in the decade leading up to the First World War. Since at least 1880, Britain, France, Germany, Austria-Hungary, and Russia had competed for colonies and dominance from East Asia to Africa. And the competition heightened tensions between these powers over long-standing disputes over European territory, in places such as the Balkans. After 1914, it was obvious to all that such conflict had been dry tinder into which the match of Archduke Franz Ferdinand's assassination was tossed, igniting general war.

Schumpeter, it happens, was acquainted with another of the most important contributors to the debate on imperialism, Rudolf Hilferding, who in 1905–6 had attended the famous Böhm-Bawerk seminar with Schumpeter. About five years later, Hilferding published *Finance Capital* (1910), his most famous work, in which he argued that imperialism was a consequence of "the Latest Phase of Capitalist Development," to use the book's subtitle. In particular, he argued first that capitalism was changing in the early twentieth century, with the development of a complex banking system and, relatedly, industrial cartels. (Thus like Schumpeter, Hilferding stressed the significance of bank credit for capitalism.) Cartels, he thought, could protect themselves during economic crises, using their market power to maintain higher prices. But this strategy could only be sustained if a tariff wall protected the domestic market from foreign competition. And since relatively high domestic prices dampened sales, cartels also sought access to foreign markets in which they could dump excess production, as well as invest excess capital. Cartels thus became strong proponents of the use of state power to capture foreign markets for these purposes—in short, proponents of imperialism. This was the Marxist theory of imperialism that Schumpeter knew. Lenin's contribution, although it may now be more famous, actually relied heavily on Hilferding's, and Schumpeter probably did not consult it before writing his own essay.[9] And Schumpeter had little to say about Rosa Luxemburg's *The Accumulation of Capital* (1913), whose argument, though similar to Hilferding's, rested more exclusively on the presumed need of capitalist nations to seek access to noncapitalist ones as venues for investment.

Schumpeter apparently set out to respond in some way to the claim that capitalism contained an inherent mechanism fostering imperialism. A puzzling aspect of Schumpeter's essay, though, is that it at first sidesteps this argument, and then ultimately accepts it, in a limited way. Instead of beginning with a denial that capitalism contained an imperialist tendency, Schumpeter began by defining the issue away. In Hilferding's view, it should be stressed, imperialist policy was perfectly rational, given the imperatives of capitalism at a particular time. But Schumpeter proceeded by defining imperialism as irrational, as "the objectless disposition on the part of a state to unlimited forcible expansion" (Schumpeter [1918–19] 1991, 143). This simply excluded from consideration the phenomenon Hilferding claimed to explain. And there is something else curious about this opening definition and the arguments that follow from it. Hilferding and other Marxists assumed that they were trying to explain a particularly modern tendency or mechanism, one unique to a particular stage of capitalism. Schumpeter adopted a quite different course, defining imperialism as a transhistorical phenomenon—one, if anything, best understood in light of its earliest occurrences in ancient Egypt, Assyria, Persia, Arabia, Greece, and Rome. There was something more at issue here, it should be noted, than the breadth of historical evidence sifted. Also relevant was whether the goal was to elucidate the structure and tendencies of a particular form of contemporary society and economy or, by contrast, to survey all the diverse societies throughout history that had engaged in similar kinds of expansionist policy. The difference is significant since it would seem unlikely that any single mechanism could serve to explain all forcible state expansion in history. Now Hilferding and other Marxists clearly thought of themselves as engaged in the former task. Their claim, that is, was that "finance" capitalism contained within it a particular mechanism that led to violent national expansion and international conflict. But they would not have claimed this mechanism was the cause of any forcible state expansion in the ancient or medieval world. By contrast, Schumpeter, in defining the outcome to be explained very broadly—"the objectless disposition on the part of a state to unlimited forcible expansion"—seems to have set himself the initial task of uncovering a wide variety of mechanisms that might lead to such broadly described state behavior.

Yet, after offering his definition of imperialism and setting himself the task of a broad survey, Schumpeter next proceeded as if his task were to locate a single "atavistic" mechanism causing imperialism. Then only after describing this mechanism did he turn directly to the causal claims of the Marxists concerning turn-of-the-century capitalism. And although he initially argued that certain crucial features of capitalism generally tended against imperialism, he did not deny that something like the Hilferding mechanism could be at work in the modern world. All this is considerably more complex and problematic than scholars usually admit. Even Richard Swedberg, who rightly points out that "Imperialisms" should not be seen as either psychologically or economically reductive argues too simply that Schumpeter's "main point" is to "reject the Marxist theory of imperialism . . . and to present an alternative theory which is more flexible and sociological in nature" (Swedberg 1991a, 50).

Turning to the actual substance of Schumpeter's atavism-centered explanation of imperialism: its first component combined his general view that social relations and beliefs tend to outlive the forces that brought them forth, with his view of elites and their specific function in different societies. "The explanation lies," he argued, "in the vital needs of situations that molded peoples and classes into warriors—if they wanted to avoid extinction—and in the fact that psychological dispositions and social structure acquired in the dim past in such situations, once firmly established, tend to maintain themselves and to continue in effect long after they have lost their meaning and their life-preserving function" (Schumpeter [1918–19] 1991, 187–8). For example, Schumpeter contended that in Egypt a "class of professional soldiers," formed during war against the Hyksos, persisted even after those wars were over—along with its "warlike instincts and interests" (157). Schumpeter capped this part of the narrative with this pithy summary of his viewpoint: "*Created by wars that required it, the machine now created the wars it required*" (157). Schumpeter ultimately argued that the same applied to more recent imperialism—that it was at least partly atavistic, attributable to the birth struggles of absolutist states, and the interests and mind-set of the aristocracy shaped by those struggles.

Having set this argument out, Schumpeter went on to argue, further, that capitalism had no affinity with *this type* of imperialism. He had essentially three reasons for this. The first was that capitalism introduced and fostered highly rationalistic habits of mind, and that these tended to dissolve all sorts of irrational, historical holdovers, including the beliefs and practices underpinning this sort of imperialism (Schumpeter [1918–19] 1991, 190–1). Another—probably the most cited argument in the essay, because it mostly closely approximates the expected direct rebuttal to Marxists—is that under capitalist free trade, "*no* class has an interest in forcible expansion as such" because in such a world, materials, capital and labor can move freely to those who can use them most profitably, and national control of any of them is irrelevant (196). Thus capitalism itself offered no incentives for imperialism. On the contrary, capitalism and those who benefited from it, needed peace in order to thrive. A third argument was that a "warrior nation," could allow little room for private life—such a nation in fact called people out of private life—while in the culture fostered by capitalism, "individual life carries its own center of gravity within itself, where its meaning lies in the individual and his personal sphere" (Schumpeter [1918–19] 1991, 158; [1918] 1991, 109). "There is much less excess energy to be vented in war and conquest than in any precapitalist society," he claimed (Schumpeter [1918–19] 1991, 191).

Now, the first and third arguments, though opposed to the general idea that capitalism was intrinsically imperialistic, were not directly aimed at Hilferding's argument, which after all did not attribute imperialism to irrationality or to the culture and ideology of capitalism, but to reputed economic imperatives. The second argument was, by contrast, more apposite. Yet Schumpeter regarded this second, economic, argument as less definitive than is sometimes thought. Even at the beginning of the essay, Schumpeter wrote that he did not doubt that the attempt "to derive imperialist tendencies from the economic-structural influences that shape life in general" would prove at least partly successful (Schumpeter [1918–19] 1991, 143). And on reflection, it should come as no surprise that Schumpeter was not led by his second argument—that under capitalist free trade, no one has an interest in imperialism—to utterly reject the Hilferding position. Schumpeter, after all, had never thought that the abstract competitive-equilibrium vision of the economy—the one that would put the most emphasis on a free trade ideal—was an adequate one. Strikingly, Schumpeter agreed with Hilferding that under conditions of tariff protection and cartelization, there was an interest in the forcible capture and protection of foreign markets. Cartelized industries, made possible by protectionism, needed to dump excess production abroad, and banks in cartelized nations were strongly motivated to channel capital abroad as well. Suddenly it mattered—although it did not before—what nation built a railroad in a developing country. "What matters is to gain a foothold of some kind and then to exploit this foothold as a base for the conquest of new markets," Schumpeter argued (201).

Schumpeter's caveats had caveats, however, for he also insisted that protectionism itself did not grow out of intrinsic mechanisms of capitalism, but was itself an atavistic holdover. In particular, Schumpeter argued that it was absolutist monarchs who originated protective tariffs for essentially private reasons, and that the bourgeoisie later simply adopted many of the prejudices of such monarchs because of the recurrent historical alliance between the rising bourgeoisie and the monarchs in Europe (Schumpeter [1918–19] 1991, 206–12). (As we will see, this view of capitalist society as an amalgam of contemporary and feudal structures was central for Schumpeter.) In any case, he argued that even when export monopolism—the combination of cartelization and protectionism—took root, most capitalistic societies would include classes—such as workers and small capitalists—who understood that their interests were opposed to imperial adventures (203–5). Thus, he argued, eventually, "imperialism will wither and die" (214).

We have then, an explanation embracing a variety of causal mechanisms—some working counter to others—and an argument making many concessions to the alternative Schumpeter is usually seen as attempting to demolish. Odd though this may seem, there is no reason to believe that Schumpeter was equivocating for political reasons. The elements of "Imperialisms" were all consistent with arguments Schumpeter made elsewhere. And for Schumpeter none of the various arguments available to him would have seemed both plausible and attractive in its political implications. Although he might have liked to offer a simple refutation of the Marxist thesis, he simply could not believe in a pure-free-trade vision of capitalism. And his own "atavism" argument offered him no comfort as a conservative concerned with the fate of the hybrid European societies he cherished. For Schumpeter thought that the feudal elements that got a substantial portion of the blame for the destructive imperialism of his time were also a crucial pillar for capitalism, as we will see below.

And he also thought the rationalist tendencies that in capitalism ought eventually to undermine imperialism were simultaneously terribly dangerous to the capitalist order.

Social Classes

There was for Schumpeter a less pressing motivation for writing "Social Classes in an Ethnically Homogenous Environment" (1927) than there had been for "Tax State" and "Imperialisms." No burning topical issue was involved, such as whether First World War sounded the death knell for the capitalist tax state, or whether the war represented a necessary and most malign side of the capitalist process. Nevertheless, the essay on class served to offer a sharply contrasting alternative to a Marxist conception.[10] And it also elaborated upon important aspects of "Crisis" and "Imperialism"—aspects whose importance might not seem clear except when read in conjunction with "Social Classes." For the decline of the feudal nobility through "patrimonialization," a key element of "Crisis," and the prominence of warrior elites, a crucial part of "Imperialisms," were only fully elaborated by means of the theory of class dynamics laid out in "Social Classes." The argument on class also had important links to *Economic Development*.

The substance of the essay can be easily summarized. According to Schumpeter, the nature and constitution of the classes in a given society and their relationship to one another could be explained primarily by the function that a class or its members played in society, in combination with the aptitude of different families to fulfill that function. "Class structure is the ranking of such individual families by their social value in accordance, ultimately, with their differing aptitudes," Schumpeter argued (Schumpeter [1927] 1991, 274). The picture was made more complex by the fact—in Schumpeter's view—that elite classes were able to consolidate their power and entrench themselves, so that a given society was a product both of present and past social needs.

In Schumpeter's historical view, class relations were products also of constant motion. In fact, class structure had to be understood in terms of three different types of movement, the movement of families within classes, the movement of families between classes, and the rise and fall of whole classes. It is easier, in some ways, to present Schumpeter's argument in a different order than he did, and to begin with the rise and fall of classes. This movement Schumpeter attributed to the ability of the class to carry out some social function. "Every class," according to Schumpeter,

> has a definite function, which it must fulfill according to its whole concept and orientation, and which it actually does discharge as a class and through the class conduct of its members. Moreover, the position of each class in the total national structure depends, on the one hand, on the significance that is attributed to that function, and, on the other hand, on the degree to which the class successfully performs the function. (Schumpeter [1927] 1991, 256)

For example, the feudal nobility owed its position, Schumpeter argued, to its ability to provide military protection, to pursue war as a way of life (Schumpeter [1927] 1991, 258–62)—a theme already familiar from "Imperialisms." By the same token, the nobility began to decline, in his view, as soon as it let slip this martial function, seeking to base its privileges on heredity instead of service in war (262–3). According to a similar argument, the capitalist bourgeoisie owed its position to its ability to engage in economic innovation. In this sense, we can now see, the argument of *Economic Development*—the view that capitalism is driven forward by entrepreneurial innovation—was not after all purely economic, but was tightly linked to a particular sociological theory of classes and their functions.

What then, of the rise and fall of families—their movement within and between classes? (Note that for Schumpeter it was families that moved, rather than just individuals.) Schumpeter attributed within-class movement to "shrewdness in the management of a given position" and the ability to carry out the designated class's function (Schumpeter [1927] 1991, 240, 240–1). As for cross-class movement, Schumpeter argued, "the family in question only needs to be near the upper or lower border line of its class, and the factors that account for shifts [within classes] to be strong enough to surmount the barriers peculiar to classes" (252).

Two methodological aspects of "Social Classes" deserve note here because they bring into sharper focus exactly what Schumpeter really meant. First, Schumpeter's argument was insistently realist, in the sense that he held—contrary to many contemporary political scientists and sociologists—that a class was not just a descriptive category but a real entity, "a special social organism, living, acting and suffering as such" ([1927] 1991, 232). Second, the unit of analysis for Schumpeter in this essay was the family, not the individual (Schumpeter [1927] 1991, 274). Indeed, for Schumpeter, this was the point of talking about class: one's fate as an individual was considerably governed by the family and class into which one was born. One should bear this in mind when assessing Schumpeter's introduction of the term "methodological individualism." The individualist method, in his view, made sense for some problems, but not for others.

Schumpeter as a Conservative Thinker

It is now possible again to deepen our understanding of Schumpeter as a political thinker. Schumpeter never wrote a unitary, systematic, book-length work of political philosophy that took readers from abstract premises to concrete applications. So what, then, marks him as a conservative thinker? The answers are to be found more than anywhere else in his narrative or explanatory account of capitalist decline, his argument that the reinforcing structures of the society he so highly valued were subject to severe strains and were unlikely to hold out. His conservatism was doubly implicated in this account of the decline of the "capitalist order." First, it underscores that Schumpeter wished to conserve what he could of the hybrid capitalist society in which he had come of age: a society in which innovation drove the capitalist system forward under the protection of traditional political leadership. Yet aspects of this social construct had already vanished irrevocably by 1920 and many more were threatened, he believed. So Schumpeter regarded the conservation of this hybrid as possible only in a very limited sense, precisely because of what he saw as the capitalist order's crumbling walls. To understand the narrative of decline and the related possibilities of conservatism is one task of the next sections. Another mark of Schumpeter's conservatism was his elaboration in the context of this account upon certain characteristic themes that have come to be associated with different varieties of conservatism. Here some caution is warranted. It might be tempting to posit a single shared theme—a principle or an idea—uniting all conservative theorists. But in truth, no such theme exists, no matter how much we may take for granted certain features of contemporary conservative political argument. For example, neither wholehearted advocacy of private enterprise nor belief in the role of religious institutions or values in stabilizing social life would qualify as inalterable tenets of conservatism. But it is possible to argue that different conservatisms bear at least a "family likeness" to each other, explainable in terms of their sharing various themes. That is, just as three members of a family may have dimples, four atrocious tempers, and two double-jointed elbows, it is likely that there is some *set* of premises, arguments, or values, each shared to various degrees by some—but never all—conservatives.

There is no need to try and list every one of these values or arguments. But it is possible to name those central elements of Schumpeter's social thought that he most obviously shared with other prominent members of the family of conservatives. One would be belief that a particular group's sociopolitical leadership—premised on unique abilities, attainments or virtues—should be recognized or promoted. A second would be strong doubts about human reason, or at least about the most ardent claims made for it. And a third would be a deep suspicion of intellectuals. It is not surprising that Edmund Burke, widely hailed as the founder of modern conservatism, happens to have shared all these family traits with Schumpeter, and is, in particular, perhaps the best example of a conservative critic of what he termed "intriguing philosophers." (Burke [1790] 1999, 419). But other notable conservatives and libertarians can be associated with each of the intellectual traits I have just mentioned—Ayn Rand for her celebration of industrialists and their natural leadership skills, for example, or Michael Oakeshott for his suspicion of "rationalism." As we continue to explore Schumpeter's thought, we shall see how each of these ideas or convictions functioned in his analytic narrative of capitalist decline, and served both to connect and distinguish him from different varieties of conservatism.

Schumpeter clearly styled himself as a conservative as early as 1916, although not in public writings. And there is good reason to believe that Schumpeter's historical ideal of conservatism partook deeply of the state of society, the economy, and politics in Europe in the decades before First World War. As we have seen, it was during the First World War that Schumpeter addressed a series of private memos to members of conservative circles—memos whose main theme, from the beginning, was how to protect and conserve the "innermost essence" of the Austro-Hungarian monarchy, its "entire domestic political structure," something that for Schumpeter meant not just the political office of the monarch, but the entire traditional, multiethnic sociopolitical body that the monarch notionally held together (Schumpeter [1916] 1985, 251, 252). It is fairly clear that what Schumpeter truly admired about this period, both in Austria-Hungary and elsewhere—was what he termed the "active symbiosis of two social strata," bourgeoisie and nobility, "one of which no doubt supported the other economically but was in turn supported by the other politically" (Schumpeter [1942] 1976, 136). For Schumpeter, it is because of this symbiosis—and not unalloyed bourgeois rule—that this was "the period of intact and vital capitalism" (136). In England, it was the period of what he termed in his secret memoranda and elsewhere "Tory democracy," a term he seemed to apply equally to the strategies and policies of the Conservative and Liberal parties of late nineteenth-century England. For Schumpeter, this signified the management of nascent democratic tendencies by the Tory or traditional conservative elements of society. And, from a variety of different angles, he devoted considerable space to interpreting what he saw as the era's sociopolitical equipoise in his political memos, in writings just after the First World War, and even as late as the 1930s and 1940s.[11] "I liked those times," Schumpeter told a Boston audience in 1941 (Schumpeter [1941] 1991, 387). And there seems little doubt that he had reveled in the aristocratic and high bourgeois milieus in which, as a boy and young man, he had enjoyed considerable personal success.[12] Yet Schumpeter's love of this era was tinctured with a sense of regret—his treatment of the period as an embodied ideal tinged with a belief that no such ideal could persist unchanged. Thus his admission that he "liked those times" was followed immediately by this: "but since there is no use in wishful thinking, I realize that that world is dead and buried and there is no way back to it" (387–8). It is in this context that we can interpret Schumpeter's fairly consistent understanding of conservatism itself as a strategy of moderating, but not preventing, social transformation. This is the overall message of the wartime memos, as well as the crux of a few clear and explicit—if not elaborate and extended—comments on the nature of conservatism. Earlier we saw his 1919 argument that the best conservative policy refused to shrink from political necessity, but accepted it with realism, creating "conservative successes on what would otherwise have become Conservative defeats" (Schumpeter [1918–19] 1991, 144). We have seen that this viewpoint shared much in common with the attitude of successive Austro-Hungarian governments, as they engaged the forces of disintegration. But Schumpeter continued to view conservatism this way, arguing more than two decades after the disappearance of the empire: "[N]o more can be achieved by individual or group volitions than to perform transitions with a minimum of loss of human values. The latter, the bringing about of transitions from your social structure to other social structures with a minimum loss of human values, that is how I should define conservatism" (Schumpeter [1941] 1991, 399). Moderating social change was then a value for Schumpeter. But equally important as this value for Schumpeter was an appropriate and clear-eyed view of the change being moderated, something he thought was contained in his discussion of capitalism's "crumbling walls."

The Capitalist Order's "Crumbling Walls"

Much of Schumpeter's narrative of capitalist decline follows from his understanding of rationality. In contemporary social science—especially, today, in political science—"rationality" has come often to designate a certain kind of private calculation in which an individual aims to maximize some desired thing (economic profits, or electoral votes, or, more abstractly, utility). We have already seen how Schumpeter viewed such theories of maximizing rationality. He countenanced the assumption of such rationality, but with limits. First, he insisted that social scientists, especially economists, should recognize that the actual people they studied were not generally engaging in rational maximization. Many, at most, were simply following traditional practices that had maximizing effects. But second, he argued that assuming such maximizing rationality was still acceptable scientific practice for pure economics. For it was a way of separating the study of the economic system from any complicating questions of culture, social practices, and beliefs—of understanding the logic of the system, the ideal relationship between different quantities. But in many cases—including, often, the study of such historical phenomena as the tax state and imperialism, where concrete questions of cultural practices and political ideologies were of primary importance—it was of no help to assume such maximizing rationality.

Separately from any evaluation of the benefits and limits of assuming maximizing rationality, Schumpeter wrote of rationality in a broader sense relevant to our discussion here. In this instance, Schumpeter was pointing to something of which rational maximization might be only an example. In this broader sense, rationality meant thinking for oneself, independently of tradition—reflecting logically on experience (Schumpeter [1942] 1976, 122).[13] Schumpeter's attitude toward rationality in this sense was also complicated. In the first place, he thought such rationality clearly characterized the action of entrepreneurs and innovators. Most importantly, such actors thought for themselves, rather than accepting and following traditional practices. And they devised solutions, drawing on logic—in a general sense—and experience. Schumpeter insisted that this sort of rationality, which could be usefully applied in all sorts of contexts, was inextricably tied to capitalism. He claimed that "it is the everyday economic task to which we as a race owe our elementary training in rational thought and behavior" (122). All the innovations of capitalism, of course, Schumpeter attributed to rationality of this kind. But it was not just commercial innovations he viewed this way. Schumpeter also credited capitalist-inspired rationality with the characteristic attitude and advancement of "modern science" (124). Moreover, in Schumpeter's view, "capitalist rationality supplied the habits of mind that evolved the methods" of the "modern hospital" and a variety of other obvious improvements in the health and well-being of society (125, 126).

We can, on the other hand, begin to grasp Schumpeter's ambivalence about this sort of rationality—and its historical dissemination in a process of "rationalization"—if we consider three disturbing possibilities that were very real to Schumpeter. The first is that there could be important, extremely valuable social institutions or practices that did not owe their power and durability to rational consideration, that rested instead on tradition, generally, or even religious or metaphysical beliefs that would be positively threatened by rational consideration of them. The second possibility was that broad, institutional rationalization could make it possible for society to do without particular individuals whose special social function was to apply rational thought to particular problems. The third was that one could err in expecting too much of rationality—or, relatedly, in expecting too much rationality from some or indeed most social actors. One could assume, incorrectly, that certain people were motivated by or even capable of rational reflection when in fact they were not. Such a concern for the ways that rationality, separated from traditional supports, could overstep itself, linked Schumpeter to such conservatives as Edmund Burke ([1790] 1999) and Michael Oakeshott ([1947] 1991), even if Schumpeter did not rely as much as these others on the idea of venerating the historical particularities and prejudices of different nations.[14] The dangers of rationalization were essential to Schumpeter's understanding of the effect of capitalism on the institutions and beliefs that support it.

At this point it is important to recall once again Schumpeter's distinction between the "capitalist system" and the "capitalist order." The "capitalist system" meant the mutually determining system of prices and quantities that was the object of study for pure economics. The "capitalist order" meant a set of surrounding institutions, beliefs, and practices that allowed the system to thrive. Schumpeter's view was that the capitalist "order" was undergoing critical and threatening changes, and it was these changes that required a conservative response.

The capitalist order for Schumpeter was a kind of composite of historical structures and social relations. It was not just the product of capitalist influences, but rather of capitalism and the bourgeoisie growing within the shelter of certain surviving feudal social relations. As early as the sixteenth century, according to Schumpeter, a pattern began to emerge in which capitalism grew, but the "steel frame" of society "consisted of the human material of feudal society and this material still behaved according to precapitalist patterns. An essentially feudal class, the nobility, filled the offices of state, officered the army, devised policies" (Schumpeter [1942] 1976, 136). In fact, according to Schumpeter, "the aristocratic element continued to rule the roost *right to the end of the period of intact and vital capitalism*" (136). (Clearly such a view motivated the Tory democracy memos during the First World War.) In Schumpeter's view, this dominance was attributable both to special ability and unique social prestige—both an ideological "halo" associated with the feudal lord, and a historically developed "ability and habit to command and to be obeyed" (137). By contrast, the bourgeoisie was not up to this sort of leadership, certainly not in terms of social prestige, or what Max Weber termed charisma. "The stock exchange is a poor substitute for the Holy Grail" Schumpeter remarked drily (137). So the "economically operative part of the bourgeois strata," according to Schumpeter "did not offer much opposition to this. On the whole, that kind of division of labor suited them and they liked it" (137).

But capitalist rationality, Schumpeter thought, was like an acid corroding this valuable composite structure. As he put it in *Capitalism, Socialism and Democracy*:

> When the habit of rational analysis of, and rational behavior in, the daily tasks of life has gone far enough, it turns back upon the mass of collective ideas and criticizes and to some extent 'rationalizes' them by way of such questions as why there should be kings and popes or subordination or tithes or property. (Schumpeter [1942] 1976, 122)

The first of the important changes threatening capitalism, then, involved what Schumpeter termed "the destruction of the protecting strata." Capitalist rationality turned against the "steel frame" that supported it, against the feudal class that provided a kind of leadership that the bourgeoisie could not. Most concretely, it attacked "the tax exemptions and the political prerogatives of the landed nobility and gentry and of the clergy" as uncongenial to the typical bourgeois citizen's "rationalist mind and to his immediate interests" (Schumpeter [1942] 1976, 135). More broadly, capitalist society, the capitalist order, Schumpeter insisted, was not "a pure reign of reason" but "the product of a force and of a discipline inculcated into the lower strata by the feudal predecessors of the business class" (Schumpeter [1941] 1991, 343). So Schumpeter argued that in undermining traditional deference the "capitalist process, both by its economic mechanics and by its psycho-sociological effects, did away with this protecting master" (Schumpeter [1942] 1976, 138–9).

There were other protective strata imperiled by capitalist development, however. In Schumpeter's view, capitalist development also undermined "the small producer and the trader," simply because there were profits to be made from eliminating such middlemen. But "the political structure of a nation is profoundly affected by the elimination of a host of small and medium-sized firms the owner-managers of which, together with their dependents, henchmen, and connections, count quantitatively at the polls and have a hold on what we may term the foreman class that no management of a large unit can ever have" (Schumpeter [1942] 1976, 140).

Capitalist development and capitalist rationality also—and even more ironically—undermined the entrepreneur, in Schumpeter's view. Schumpeter had always stressed that one should not simply identify the social function of innovation with particular individuals. First, he always argued that even the most creative of capitalists did not innovate all the time or for their whole lives. And increasingly, throughout his career, he also argued that innovation was something that could be carried out by groups and institutions rather than individuals. Today, we might think of the research and development apparatuses of large corporations, such as pharmaceutical companies, and their interconnections with government-sponsored programs and subsidization. Schumpeter hinted at this as early as 1920–1 (Schumpeter 1920–1, 317). He went much further in describing the "obsolescence of the entrepreneurial function" over two decades later in *Capitalism, Socialism and Democracy*:

> This social function is already losing importance and is bound to lose it at an accelerating rate in the future . . . [I]nnovation itself is being reduced to routine. Technological progress is increasingly becoming the business of teams of trained specialists who turn out what is required and make it work in predictable ways. (Schumpeter [1942] 1976, 132)

This bureaucratization and routinization of innovation meant that technical-economic change could take place without the "romance" or "flash of genius" associated with the entrepreneur. More importantly, according to Schumpeter, it shook the social structure. Not all members of the bourgeoisie were entrepreneurs, Schumpeter thought, but the whole bourgeois class essentially derived its social position—remember the argument of "Social Classes"—from the function so ably carried out by a few innovating class members. "To sum up this part of our argument," Schumpeter wrote,

> if capitalist evolution—"progress"—either ceases or becomes completely automatic, the economic basis of the industrial bourgeoisie will be reduced eventually to wages such as are paid for current administrative work. (Schumpeter [1942] 1976, 134)

And without a distinct bourgeois class or a distinct entrepreneurial function, key defensible barriers to socialism would collapse. Firms in which innovation had been made routine and bureaucratic could arguably be socialized. And there would be no distinct class deriving its income, its prestige, and its social position from innovation to fight this.

Schumpeter, then, argued that capitalist development undermined the class structure and forms of leadership that kept capitalism alive, while simultaneously weakening crucial values, practices, and beliefs. But culturally and intellectually, he thought capitalism did more than undermine its own supports; he thought it unleashed philosophies and arguments that directly attacked it. Here we come to Schumpeter's "sociology of the intellectual." The nub of the matter is that in Schumpeter's view, every society had intellectuals of some sort, but capitalism produced more than the usual number of discontented ones, while at the same time it lacked the means to discipline them. Premodern intellectuals, relatively few in number anyway, had been obliged to rely on feudal patrons, Schumpeter thought. They could lose their livelihoods if they failed to use their talents to support the powerful. Their latter day counterparts, however, could cultivate broader audiences and rely upon the fact that "any attack on intellectuals must run up against the private fortresses of bourgeois business which, or some of which, will shelter the quarry" (Schumpeter [1942] 1976, 150). Thus in a "bourgeois regime," Schumpeter argued, "troops may fire on strikers, but the police cannot round up intellectuals or must release them forthwith" (150). Schumpeter also argued that capitalism led to a great expansion of higher education, and this promoted the creation of a large set of unemployed intellectuals. The result was that a large number of people tended to "drift" into the life of the intellectual in a "thoroughly discontented frame of mind" (153). Some joined up with the labor movement, "imparting a revolutionary bias to the most bourgeois trade-union practices" and (here one must recall Schumpeter's view that "the mass of people never develops definite opinions on its own") turning the movement "into something that differs substantially what it would be without them" (145, 154). In Schumpeter's view, they also joined the state agencies that would eventually become socialist bureaucracies.

Related to this narrative of rationalization and capitalist decline, Schumpeter also took up the topic of democracy—in this case, democracy as an ideological solvent acting on key elements of the capitalist order. The topic is important, of course, not only because it appears to be an integral part of Schumpeter's historical narrative of capitalist decline, but also because Schumpeter's best known contribution to political philosophy is his theory of democracy as "method." Scholars who have interpreted Schumpeter's political thought generally separate the theory of democracy as "method" from the passages and comments I discuss here, passing over them while discussing democracy as "method," or treating them only as side issues. In any case, in the context of Schumpeter's discussion of capitalist decline, it is important to note that as early as the First World War, he was referring to democracy as a set of beliefs that endangered conservative institutions and practices.[15] The very term "Tory democracy" contained within itself an implied inner tension, referring, as it did, not just to a conservative strategy, but also to the democratic strains that strategy was meant to manage. But what were these strains? Schumpeter described them according to the pattern established by his general discussion of rationalization. Indeed, in several places, he referred to the "rationalizing, leveling, mechanizing, and democratizing effects of capitalist evolution" as if it were fairly clear that these things belonged and acted together (Schumpeter 1939, 697; 1920–1, 318). More specifically, Schumpeter seems in these passages to have regarded democracy—or democratic ideology—as an example of rationalization run amok, rational critique undermining traditional social relations, rationalist philosophy expecting too much of the mass of citizens. The democratic ideology that concerned Schumpeter was "a product of early capitalism"—and displayed this provenance in its emphasis on "the rational and hedonistic individual and his ethical autonomy" (Schumpeter [1942] 1976, 248, 249). According to Schumpeter: "The ideology of democracy as reflected by the classical doctrine rests on a rationalist scheme of human action and of the values of life . . . [H]istorically, the modern democracy rose along with capitalism, and in causal connection with it" (296). Rationalist dissent was almost intrinsically egalitarian, democratic dissent. And this combined rationalist-democratic threat was dangerously broad. Schumpeter wrote:

> Formerly when people were dissatisfied with a pope or a king, they would revolt against the particular pope or king, but they took the institution for granted. Now we ask ourselves, 'Why should there be such things as popes or kings?' The bourgeois asked this question. It did not strike him that the same question would be answered unfavorably to the capitalist. (Schumpeter [1941] 1991, 360)

With both capitalist and premodern elites losing their reasons for protecting the capitalist system, and with a fifth column of intellectuals to stir up opposition among the working class, the capitalist order was deeply imperiled, in Schumpeter's view.

Exactly what he thought anyone should do about this is a vexed question, and one surprisingly few scholars have addressed.

Democracy

Among students of politics, Schumpeter is known more for *Capitalism, Socialism and Democracy* than for any other work. And in fact he is known more for just the four chapters of that book addressing the meaning and nature of democracy than for the whole surrounding narrative of economic and sociopolitical change. The reputation of these chapters—the fact that they have been admitted to the scholarly canon as a stand-alone contribution to the definition of democracy—is a testament to the vigor of Schumpeter's writing, and to his ability to make novel contributions seemingly far from his field of expertise. The chapters on democracy have most often been treated as a scholarly effort to arrive at a definition of democracy that is realistic—harmonious with stylized observations about existing regimes that were generally reckoned to be democratic. That is, many interpreters accept that Schumpeter fit the model of the politically detached university professor, and assume that he thought the question of democracy's definition could be addressed, separately from other sociopolitical problems, simply in light of the "facts" of contemporary democracies. But Schumpeter himself emphasized that his interest in democracy grew directly out of his deep concern about what he perceived as capitalism's decline: "The problem of democracy forced its way into the place it now occupies in this volume because it proved impossible to state my views on the relation between the socialist order of society"—a form of society he thought quite likely to develop in capitalism's place—"and the democratic method of government without a rather extensive analysis of the latter" (Schumpeter [1942] 1947, xiii). And we shall soon see that Schumpeter's definition—and its claimed fidelity to democratic reality—are less interesting than the various conceptual claims and sociopolitical arguments upon which it rested.

The language Schumpeter used in explaining his motive, emphasizing "the democratic method of government," also points to the accepted centerpiece of the chapters: Schumpeter's elite conception of democracy as a "method." According to this conception, democracy was best seen as a means, not an end, a set of institutions that allowed elite political agents to compete for the support of mass voters in elections. This conception of democracy, then, downplayed values that have often been associated with democracy—especially political freedom and participation—and treated democracy as a form of elite political rule.

Schumpeter laid the groundwork for this theory of democracy primarily by criticizing and rebutting what he understood to be the chief alternative views. Thus, after briefly canvassing the beliefs and practices of socialists concerning democracy, he criticized the idea that democracy could simply be understood as "rule of the people." The second half of this expression—"the people"—clarified nothing, he argued, because any decision about who was included in the suffrage always implied some exclusions. "The people" could mean a group as narrow or broad as any "people" themselves liked (Schumpeter [1942] 1976, 243–5). And since "rule" could never be absolute, the entire expression had in fact to be jettisoned, Schumpeter wrote.

But if the people could not rule directly, could they rule in some modified way through representatives? Schumpeter denied it: "only a (physical or moral) person can legally delegate or be represented"—a people could not (Schumpeter [1942] 1976, 248). The political theory of representation, he insisted, was the shoddy product of a "legal mind," which "ransacked the lumber room of its constructs" for a way to make it seem that existing arrangements amounted to popular rule (247). Parliaments were simply government organs, like courts or bureaucracies, not representative bodies. Interestingly, these comments show that Schumpeter's writings stand in more complex relation to debates about representation and representative institutions than is sometimes thought. In a recent book, for example, Nadia

Urbinati refers to the "traditional defense of representative institutions" by "Schumpeterian and neo-Schumpeterian theorists" (Urbinati 2006, 4). But Schumpeter insisted on the impossibility of representation, even while embracing what are usually understood today to be "representative" institutions (elections, mass parties, and parliaments) as the only possible realizations of anything like democracy.

From criticizing the conceptions popular rule and representation, Schumpeter proceeded to criticize the "eighteenth century" theory that in democracy, the "will of the people" would naturally gravitate toward the "common good" (Schumpeter [1942] 1976, 250). First, like Hayek and a good many others, Schumpeter insisted that there simply was no "common" good. He meant that there was no "uniquely determined common good that all people could agree on or be made to agree on by the force of rational argument" (251). The problem was, first, that the "common good" necessarily meant different things to different people. But more than this, no "rational argument" could reconcile these different views, because they were based on "irreducible differences of ultimate values" (251). Here Schumpeter adopted one version of a general type of argument that has reappeared in a variety of forms in the last century: sometimes as the claim that facts, but never values, can be discussed rationally; sometimes as the claim that worldviews are both so encompassing and so divergent that it is impossible for different people raised in one culture to understand another; or sometimes as the claim that scientific change consists only of a succession of incommensurable "paradigms" for viewing the world, with no neutral criteria for assessing whether one of these paradigms is better. Such arguments have been extremely varied in their scope and the field of their application. Schumpeter's point was essentially political. He claimed that any attempt to compromise or adjudicate between the values that motivated people in politics could only "maim and degrade" those values (251)—a pessimistic position, indeed about the possibilities of either democracy or political pluralism.

Schumpeter interpreted use of the expression "the will of the people" to indicate belief in an intrinsic rational capacity on the part of the public, in general, to decide how to act politically, and confidence that this capacity would tend to draw the public toward a decision in harmony with the "common good." So because he had rebutted the idea of the "common good" already, Schumpeter could have argued that he had disposed of the conception of the "will of the people" as well. But in fact, he offered another more direct critique of the idea of a common rational capacity. First he doubted that "individual volition"—upon which any "will of the people" would have to be built—could be relied upon. He argued that the idea of "a definite will that is the prime mover of action" had been steadily fading in light of disillusioning evidence from a variety of fields (Schumpeter [1942] 1976, 256). In their roles as economic consumers, for example, individuals could not live up to "textbook" standards: "their wants are nothing like as definite and their actions upon those wants nothing like as rational and prompt" as standard economic theory presumed (257). (I have referred to this view of Schumpeter's already, in dealing with his approach to equilibrium economics, and again, with respect to capitalist decline.) And when public, political, rather than personal issues were at stake, matters were worse. Here most people exhibited a "reduced sense of reality" and a "reduced sense of responsibility" as well as "the absence of effective volition" (261). Citizens had "wishes," "daydreams," "grumbles," "likes and dislikes" but not political "will," or what Schumpeter termed "the psychic counterpart of purposeful responsible action" (261). For this reason, individual citizens were easy prey for ideological manipulation. "Dark urges" could easily be seized upon by the unscrupulous (262). And both agitators and professional politicians could seize on the weakness of will, which allowed them "to fashion, and within very wide limits, even to create the will of the people" (263). The picture only got worse when the combination of individual wills was taken into account—when people acted in or as a group or when individual opinions were, in any manner, aggregated. At best, in light of

Schumpeter's argument for the absence of any "common good," the mechanical adding-up of intrinsically irreconcilable individual wills would yield "results" that "would not, except by chance, be meaningful in themselves" (253). Worse, research on the "psychology of crowds" showed that "human behavior when under the influence of agglomeration" was characterized by "the sudden disappearance, in a state of excitement, of moral restraints and civilized modes of thinking and feeling, the sudden eruption of primitive impulses, infantilisms and criminal propensities" (257). This was true not only of actual mobs, but of any group. "Every parliament, every committee, every council of war composed of a dozen generals in their sixties, displays, in however mild a form, some of those features that stand out so glaringly in the case of the rabble," Schumpeter argued (257). This was why he concluded that "the electoral mass" was "incapable of action other than a stampede" (283).[16]

In parallel with these arguments, Schumpeter presented the case that democracy must be regarded as a "method"—a means and not an end in itself. The argument deserves some close attention. Under the heading of "A Mental Experiment," Schumpeter began as follows: "Suppose that a community, in a way which satisfies the reader's criteria of democracy, reached the decision to persecute religious dissent" (Schumpeter [1942] 1976, 240). After several paragraphs contending that notable democratic communities throughout history had in fact engaged in such practices, Schumpeter picked up the line of argument again: "Let us transport ourselves into a hypothetical country that, in a democratic way, practices the persecution of Christians, the burning of witches, and the slaughtering of Jews" (242). Schumpeter then considered this situation from the standpoint of two implied distinctions, between method and outcome, and between adherence to democracy versus adherence to other valued things. He wrote:

> We should certainly not approve of these [persecutory] practices on the ground that they have been decided on according

> to the rules of democratic procedure. But the crucial question is: would we approve of the democratic constitution itself that produced such results in preference to a non-democratic one that would avoid them? (242)

Schumpeter's point was that a reasonable democrat—one, in this case, who recognized the value of freedom of religion—would have to disapprove of the persecution, even while approving of the democratic method by which it was decided to persecute. Such a democrat would have to recognize, then, that the outcome was objectionable, even though the method was democratic, and that there were values that weigh more heavily at times than the mere following of a democratic method. As he put it:

> There are ultimate ideals and interests which the most ardent democrat will put above democracy, and all he means if he professes uncompromising allegiance to it is that he feels convinced that democracy will guarantee those ideals and interests such as freedom of conscience and speech, justice, decent government and so on. The reason why this is so is not so far to seek. Democracy is a political *method*, that is to say, a certain type of institutional arrangement for arriving at political—legislative and administrative—decisions and hence incapable of being an end in itself, irrespective of what decisions it will produce under given historical conditions. (Schumpeter [1942] 1976, 242)

A difficulty with this argument can be approached by asking: why should we accept in the first place that religious persecution could be considered democratic? One could easily argue that democracy must entail or include the respect for rights that religious persecution necessarily violates.[17] Yet Schumpeter did not argue against or even consider this possibility. Instead, it is clear, from the beginning and indeed, throughout, that he regarded democracy simply as a decision-making method that involved some application of majority rule. In other words it was a presupposition, an initial stipulation of Schumpeter's—not the conclusion of his argument, as he claimed—that persecution could be carried out *democratically* if it was a course chosen according to certain minimal procedures. For throughout the passage, and not only at the end, Schumpeter used such expressions as "in a democratic way," and "according to the rules of democratic procedure" (Schumpeter [1942] 1976, 242).

At last we may turn to Schumpeter's definition, the focus of almost all considerations of his democratic theory. That is, we are ready to answer the question: if democracy is a "method," and if that method cannot involve "rule by the people," "common good," or "will of the people," what, precisely, is the "democratic method?" His answer was this: "the democratic method is that institutional arrangement for arriving at political decisions in which individuals acquire the power to decide by means of a competitive struggle for the people's vote" (Schumpeter [1942] 1976, 269). This definition has at least four important implications for conceptualizing democracy.

The first distinguishable conceptual element of Schumpeter's argument about democracy, then, was the emphasis on elite rule. "This definition," he wrote, "leaves all the room we may wish to have for a proper recognition of the vital fact of leadership" (Schumpeter [1942] 1976, 270). Since "collectives act almost exclusively by accepting leadership," he insisted, democracy could be defined not as popular rule but as "the rule of the politician" (270, 285). Democracy was then, like any other possible political arrangement, a kind of elite rule. It was unique only in that its leadership group was composed of professional politicians, rather than warlords or priests. The chapter in which Schumpeter offered his definition thus included a number of appreciative reviews of the skills and energy of professional politicians. Schumpeter insisted that recognition of democracy as rule of the politician meant that certain democratic ideas—or perhaps, more properly, we should term them "republican" ideas, in the historical sense of that term—valorizing citizenship and amateurism in politics had to be put to rest. Success in politics required "concentration of the professional kind"; it "will unavoidably be a career," he said (285). And a further implication of this, Schumpeter said, was clear. There was a "distinct professional interest in the individual politician" and "a distinct group interest in the political profession as such" (285). Thus, just as functioning markets did not rely on producers seeking directly to provide society with the things needed to thrive, so too functioning democratic politics did not rely on politicians aiming to provide good laws and good government. Instead, "the democratic method produces legislation and administration as by-products of the struggle for political office" (286).

With this, our discussion has taken us to the second key conceptual element of Schumpeter's "definition" of democracy, the electoral competition among elites or "the struggle for political office" that Schumpeter saw as the engine propelling democracy. "Competition for leadership"—"free competition for a free vote"—was to "define democracy," according to Schumpeter (Schumpeter [1942] 1976, 271). But for Schumpeter—never, as we have seen, one to let ideal market models serve as more than ideal reference points—political competition was no less prone to imperfection, even fraud, than was economic competition. Legitimate democratic competition could not be said to include military coups, but the term did not "exclude cases that are strikingly analogous to the economic phenomena we label 'unfair' or 'fraudulent' competition or restraint of competition" (271).

Yet another conceptual element to Schumpeter's elite conception of democracy as method was a corollary of the first mentioned: the downplaying of mass participation in democracy. "The classical theory . . . attributed to the electorate an altogether unrealistic degree of initiative," Schumpeter said (Schumpeter [1942] 1976, 270). The classical theory was unrealistic, Schumpeter maintained, because it failed to account for the frailties of reason and will he had discussed. And in light of these frailties, Schumpeter insisted not only that the electorate *was* passive, but that it *should* be. "The voters outside of parliament must respect the division of labor between themselves and the politicians they elect," he wrote:

> They must not withdraw confidence too easily between elections and they must understand that, once they have elected an individual, political action is his business and not theirs. This means that they must refrain from instructing him about what he is to do [and even from] . . . bombarding them with letters and telegrams. (295)[18]

Finally, it should be clear that one of the main points of Schumpeter's critique of the "classical doctrine" and his offering of the method-centered alternative was to excise from the meaning of democracy any reference to what he understood to be traditionally democratic values. This is already obviously true of "rule by the people" and "common good." These were clearly no more than empty phrases, in his view. Schumpeter also argued that the "relation between democracy and freedom is not absolutely stringent and can be tampered with" (Schumpeter [1942] 1976, 272), an idea fully consistent with his willingness to conceive of "democratic" persecution and his actually favoring the limitation of constituent contacts with legislators. Relatedly—and based on his dismissal of the idea of "the people" as meaningless—he also contended that widespread citizen participation had little to do with democracy. Exclusions from suffrage based on gender, race, economic status, and religion were arguably "compatible with democracy" (244–5). "Fitness" after all, "is a matter of opinion," he argued (244). And given Schumpeter's assumptions about ordinary people's agency—his deprecation of will—there was little ground for concern about whether ordinary people could find in democracy much outlet for political action and expression.

How does this elite conception of democracy relate to the conservative elements of Schumpeter's social, economic, and political thought? This is a surprisingly difficult question, the response to which has implications for what one understands Schumpeter to have meant and intended in writing about democracy. The best course, given the difficulties, is to lay out the different approaches that have been adopted by followers and interpreters of Schumpeter.

First, the majority of scholars who have focused attention on Schumpeter's elite conception of democracy have assumed that there was no meaningful connection to his conservatism. They have tended to see Schumpeter in their own self-image and have regarded the chapters on democracy as constituting a neutral scholarly treatise on democracy, a viewpoint supported by Schumpeter's insistence that he was seeking a "realistic" theory "independently of wishes." This has implications both for how one views the elite theory of democracy and Schumpeter's conservatism, generally. On the one hand, it implies that Schumpeter's writings on democracy may be assimilated to the category of social-scientific inquiries motivated, more or less, by the prevailing norms of social science. Many scholars have thus assumed that the comparison with political facts provides the best axis from which to assess Schumpeter's elite definition of democracy—as well as the "classical" doctrine he criticized.[19] If we view Schumpeter's elite theory of democracy this way then, ironically, the part of Schumpeter's writings that most squarely discusses a conventional political topic would have to be seen as apolitical. The elite theory, then, could never be of much interest to conservatives or indeed to any practitioners of what is sometimes termed "normative" (evaluative, ethically attuned) political theory. The intellectual and historical origin of the elite conception, its affinities and conflicts with other theories, especially normative ones, its implications for practical action—all these would matter little in comparison to its ability to predict or account for facts about politics. Such a view would also strongly suggest that Schumpeter's conservatism itself, however real it might have been to him psychologically, was essentially personal, a private mood. This interpretation is very difficult to sustain, however, because of the need to sharply separate Schumpeter's elite conception of democracy from his efforts as a conservative and from the conservative themes running through his broad historical narrative of capitalist decline. In later chapters, I shall attempt to explain the reasons why this general approach to interpreting Schumpeter became so prevalent, and demonstrate that even the elite conception of democracy, treated in isolated, contains intrinsic elements of Schumpeter's conservatism.

A second possible interpretation, embraced by a number of scholars, is that Schumpeter's elite conception of democracy functionally serves conservative purposes. But this can be seen primarily as an effect of the theory, rather than a reflection of Schumpeter's intentions. Scholars have argued that adopting the Schumpeterian view of democracy tends to make it appear that nothing more could be asked or expected of democracy than what already exists in countries from the United States to India.[20] According to this interpretation, the Schumpeterian approach, by linking democracy to elite rule, cut off possible avenues of democratic criticism, and undermined possible forms of democratic change.

A third possible type of interpretation would not necessarily challenge the view that Schumpeter's elite theory of democracy itself is most adequately assessed according to whether it fits certain "facts" of contemporary politics. But this approach would see Schumpeter's conservatism implicated either in his particular motivation for selecting democracy as a subject matter, or in the themes and assumptions out of which Schumpeter built his elite theory of democracy. Although few interpreters have stressed such an approach, the evidence for it would seem fairly solid. Schumpeter's own unambiguous explanation of why he took up democratic theory was that he wanted to say something about the nature of the socialist society toward which (he concluded on the basis of his theory of capitalist decline) the Western world seemed to be tending. Particularly, he wanted to answer the question, could socialism be democratic? Socialists, he thought, generally said yes; socialism would be the "very ideal of democracy" (Schumpeter [1942] 1976, 236). But he did not share the values or assumptions behind this claim, and it was not the only prominent view: "the reader cannot but be familiar with at least some of the numerous pamphlets that have been published in this country during the last few years in order to prove that a planned economy, let alone full-fledged socialism, is completely incompatible with democracy" (284). Although Hayek had not yet published *The Road to Serfdom* (a book Schumpeter would review unfavorably) he had published a sort of pamphlet-form version, under the title *Freedom and the Economic System*, and it seems clear that Schumpeter was referring to this and similar works. Schumpeter thought that Hayek's approach was not only wrong, but that stressing the claim that socialism could not be democratic prevented conservatives (and indeed others) from recognizing how likely it was that capitalist societies would become socialistic. What was needed, said Schumpeter, was:

> a more realistic theory of the relation that may exist between socialism and democracy themselves, that is to say, of the relation that may exist, independently of wishes and slogans, between the socialist order as we have defined it and the modus operandi of democratic government. In order to solve this problem we must first inquire into the nature of democracy. (235–6)

After examining Schumpeter's view of democracy's nature, it is possible to understand his answer to this question. Democratic socialism was certainly possible, and it meant only a combination of state ownership of the means of production with minimal democratic institutions—such as competitive elections—all enabling "rule by the politician." That Schumpeter's theory of democracy had at least this relationship to his narrative of capitalist decline (and thus in a way, to his conservatism) is not generally disputed, even though the matter is usually passed over in silence.

It is also not difficult to see that Schumpeter's elite theory of democracy developed a number of the classically conservative themes he treated elsewhere, most notably doubts about rationality, and insistence on the importance of social leadership. (I shall discuss this in Chapter 4.) As for doubts about rationality, we have seen that this was a complex and difficult topic, touching on important issues of capitalism's maintenance and decline. The problem, in Schumpeter's view, was that most people's capacity to judge social and political matters autonomously, based on their own experience, was limited. The weakness of "classical" theories of democracy, then, was the expectation that rationality could play a positive role in the formation of the "will of the people" and that this will could home in on something called the "common good." Any such rationality as politics might exhibit would have to come from the skill and action of professional politicians, the true rulers of democracy, in Schumpeter's view.

The fourth possible interpretive approach, the most controversial, would treat Schumpeter's elite theory of democracy as programmatically conservative—as directed toward conservatives who might be able to draw upon it for planning conservative action. The questions then would be: to what degree did Schumpeter actually see a clear way forward for conservatives, and how tightly connected was the elite conception of democracy to arguments he made when he clearly was claiming that some particular conservative group should act in a particular way?

For example, Schumpeter's arguments about the role of elites in democracy—and in the future democratic socialism he anticipated—were clearly linked to the particular claim, outlined above, that capitalist societies were hybrids, combining an entrepreneurial economic engine with a feudal, aristocratic skeleton. Schumpeter was convinced that contemporary social stability rested upon the acceptance of traditional leadership. But Schumpeter's elite theory of democracy pushed beyond this to the most general, abstract version of such a viewpoint in his entire body of work. Whereas in earlier political and sociological writings he identified the particular elite that was prominent in some historical form of society, in his arguments about democracy he provided just the general claims—claims about the limited understanding and skills of most citizens—that made it seem evident that democracy, too, had to be led, even dominated, by elites. That is, he argued that all societies—even notionally democratic ones—were sustained, nurtured, and directed by elites. The next question should be fairly evident. If Schumpeter thought that all societies had to be led by elites—if he thought that capitalist society would soon be replaced in many nations by democratic socialist society—did he have a prediction about who would fulfill that future elite role? Did he even concern himself with this question? It is possible to argue that Schumpeter had in fact been concerned with finding and cultivating elites to lead democratizing societies since the time he wrote the "Tory democracy" memos, and that the crucial chapters of *Capitalism, Socialism and Democracy* were motivated, in part, by similar concerns.[21] Recall that Schumpeter had addressed those memos to Austro-Hungarian aristocrats whom he hoped would organize themselves more energetically to lead and dominate the increasingly democratic political life of the empire. A similar, continuing concern for elite leadership would seem to animate Schumpeter's observation that "socialism has no obvious solution to offer for the problem solved in other forms of society by the presence of a political class of stable traditions" (Schumpeter [1942] 1976, 302). The implication would seem to be that although Schumpeter shared with some conservatives a conviction that societies needed the leadership of skilled, traditional elites, he was uncertain where such an elite would be found in the future.

Another clear and programmatic connection between Schumpeter's conservatism and these chapters on democracy can be seen in their culmination in an argument against economic democracy. This is rarely discussed by interpreters, but it is so obvious a feature of the chapters on democracy that it would seem strange to term highlighting it controversial. When Schumpeter finally arrives at the apparent end of his inquiry, the subject of "Democracy in the Socialist Order," we expect an elaboration on his conclusion, already stated, that socialism can be democratic. But Schumpeter seems to have regarded this as sufficiently clear already. Instead, more than half of this section consists of an impassioned argument against economic democracy. Now, most readers of *Capitalism, Socialism and Democracy* are probably not surprised to learn that Schumpeter was opposed to the democratization of the workplace or of direct democratic participation in economic decision-making. But what has apparently eluded many interpreters is that Schumpeter considered economic democracy a real threat worth discussing, a possible outcome of existing historical tendencies, and not just a marginal pipedream. And the reality of this threat for him led him to make one of the clearest programmatic statements in *Capitalism, Socialism and Democracy*: "No responsible person can view with equanimity the consequences of extending the democratic method . . . to all economic affairs" (Schumpeter [1942] 1976, 299). He contended that "the agencies that are to operate the economic engine" under democratic socialism "may be so organized and manned as to be sufficiently exempt in the fulfillment of their current duties from interference by politicians, or, for that matter, by fussing citizens' committees or by their workmen" (299). This is one of the most peculiar aspects of Schumpeter's rearguard conservatism: it stresses not an argument intended to defeat or fend off socialism, but an argument for maintaining elite dominance within it.[22]

* * *

There have been very few social scientists who could claim contributions so manifold and diverse as Schumpeter's. Yet although it is clear that he offered insights and striking conjectures related both to and through a compelling (if not always convincing) account of historical change, the practical significance and impact of his thought cannot be taken as given based simply on what he wrote. We must now turn to two questions that are to some degree distinct from those we have considered to this point: how Schumpeter was interpreted and used by later scholars—and why he was drawn on in this manner.

3

Influence

There is no shortage of testimonials to Joseph Schumpeter's influence. Anthony Downs, a renowned scholar in his own right, wrote that "Schumpeter's profound analysis of democracy" formed the "inspiration and foundation" for his own important work, adding that his "debt and gratitude" to Schumpeter were "great indeed" (Downs 1957, 29 n. 11). The historian Arno Mayer drew heavily on Schumpeter's work in his seminal book, *The Persistence of the Old Regime*, in which he enthused that Schumpeter's analysis of European social structure before 1914 went "beyond Marx," "beyond Weber," and "beyond Veblen" (Mayer 1981, 133). An admirer of Schumpeter's innovation theory even called him "Today's hottest economist"—in 2000, fifty years after his death (Whalen 2000).

Yet it is actually surprisingly difficult to assess the influence of a thinker as protean as Schumpeter—to assess it both realistically and with sensitivity to the complex interactions and juxtapositions that may be found whenever we trace the spread of concepts and arguments. Testimonials such as those above are easy enough to dig up. And since many writers and thinkers are forgotten almost immediately upon their deaths, let alone six decades later, the mere existence of so many heartfelt expressions of inspiration tells us that Schumpeter is in a very select group of intellectuals. But it is important not to base the evaluation of Schumpeter's place in various fields entirely on those who have cited him enthusiastically, while ignoring those writing about the same subjects who have not been affected by his work. What is needed is a thorough analysis of the extent of his influence and of the manner in which his theories, conceptions, frameworks, narratives, and approaches have motivated writing, thinking, and research during the last six decades. For beyond the question *whether* these ideas have been influential, there are of course the questions of *how* they have been influential, and *why*. And in Schumpeter's case, in addition, there is the specific question of his influence *as a conservative*, which is of particular importance for this study.

The specific nature of Schumpeter's influence on later thinkers, I contend in the next pages, has been shaped by a series lags, gaps, or disjunctures between the circumstances under which he formulated his social thought and the circumstances under which most others read and responded to it. The general effect of these temporal, spatial, and attitudinal divides has been that Schumpeter usually has been known less for the broad conservatively inspired historical narrative into which all of his social thought fit than for specific concepts and arguments abstracted from that narrative by scholars with widely differing aims and interests. My first task, then, is to describe these lags and their effects. This requires an understanding of developments both in the social world at large and within the confines of the academy. Next, in the latter parts of this chapter, I explore the impact of Schumpeterian ideas in the separate and unusually diverse fields in which he made seminal contributions. The tracing of each of these contributions' effects over time in fields from entrepreneurship to fiscal policy yields rich material that is both intrinsically fascinating and revealing of the interplay between political history and social-scientific development.

Schumpeter, Hayek, and Polanyi on the Prospects of Capitalism and Socialism

One way to understand the disjunctures to which I have referred is to consider three well-known works published during the Second

World War, all by emigrés from Central Europe to the English-speaking world, and all arguing that deep forces were transforming or threatening capitalism. Schumpeter's *Capitalism, Socialism and Democracy*, Friedrich von Hayek's *The Road to Serfdom*, and Karl Polanyi's *The Great Transformation* all remain classics in their own right, while clearly reflecting in their similarities the deep historical problems of the time in which they were written. Yet they are rarely considered together, as they should be.

Hayek published *The Road to Serfdom* in 1944 in England. But he was born in Vienna at the turn of the century to a family of ennobled civil servants and scholars. After serving in the First World War, studying with Wieser and then with Mises, and directing an institute for business cycle research, he had been hired by the London School of Economics, where he became engaged in debates about the viability of socialism. The general purpose of *The Road to Serfdom* was to warn a wartime English audience of his belief that any kind of "collectivism" would lead liberal capitalist societies toward totalitarianism. By "collectivism" he meant the use of centralized economic planning, the pursuit of a "unitary" goal for an entire society, and the related refusal (as he saw it) to acknowledge certain strictly autonomous realms for individuals, especially in economic life. More pointedly, Hayek's claim was that insofar as socialism was a type of "collectivism," socialist ideas and policies in Germany had paved the way for the Nazis. The argument was historical in broad, narrative strokes, although not in terms of meticulous attention to recovering the actual ideologies, aims, and choices of political actors. Hayek believed there had been a steady Western progression toward greater individual freedom, from the Renaissance onward. But in his view this progress had been interrupted during and after First World War, a period when, as we have seen, there was in fact great deal of attention paid to "socialist" policies and ideas of various kinds.

Karl Polanyi published *The Great Transformation: The Political and Economic Origins of Our Time* in the same year that an English public saw *The Road to Serfdom.* Born in Vienna, as Hayek was, but closer in age to Schumpeter, Polanyi had served in the

Austro-Hungarian army in First World War and later had to flee communist Hungary and fascist Austria before eventually settling at Bennington College in Vermont. In one sense, *The Great Transformation* was an attempt radically to undermine the viewpoint (promoted by Hayek and others) that markets and the exchange of commodities were natural, while attempts to regulate them were artificial and dangerous infringements on human freedom. Polanyi argued that the creation of markets for land and labor, in particular, had been the planned and coercive product of state action—most importantly separating peasants from land and livelihood. Meanwhile, regulation and welfare arrangements had arisen as a spontaneous human response to markets and commodification, an attempt by women and men to defend their well-being, their cultures and their ways of life. The dramatic interaction of these two impulses—Polanyi called it the "double movement"—had played out over centuries. In a sense, Polanyi, like Hayek, saw similarities between fascism and communism. Both were responses to what Polanyi termed "nineteenth century civilization" (Polanyi [1944] 2001, 3), by which he meant the era in which "self-regulating" markets reigned. But while Hayek saw both movements as almost inexplicable turnings from that era's promise, Polanyi saw them as responses to its failure. And while for Hayek, fascism, communism, and socialism were fundamentally the same in rejecting capitalism, Polanyi saw communism and fascism as alike only in rejecting democracy. Fascism, for Polanyi, was actually an attempt to save the market system by means of the "extirpation" of democracy and its replacement with a "political religion" (245, 249).

Schumpeter's *Capitalism, Socialism and Democracy,* we recall, comprised his most extensive attempt to advance the case that capitalism was deteriorating socially and culturally despite its intrinsic economic strengths. The tendency toward rationalization fostered by capitalism itself, he argued, would strike at the dynamic heart of the economic system and eat away at the remnant feudal institutions that protected it, enabling the rise of socialism.

The political, social, economic, and military conditions of the years in which Schumpeter's, Hayek's, and Polanyi's books were conceived and published contributed to important common features. First, all three books were shaped by the most destructive and inhumane war the world had ever seen, a war in which the modern tendencies toward all-encompassing, unconstrained violence were most horrifyingly realized. This gave all three works a palpable sense of the social world as characterized by grave danger and precipitous change. All three authors, then, took seriously the idea that social forms and institutions change and are replaced, and in particular that liberal capitalism might radically transform or be superseded. But this was not just the influence of wartime risks. Hayek, Polanyi, and Schumpeter all saw the war itself as either an episode or a culmination of a longer tempestuous period, what the historian E. J. Hobsbawm (1994, 6) has termed the "age of catastrophe," beginning with the First World War, and continuing through world depression. In fact, all three were deeply interested in what they took to be even longer term historical developments in Western societies. The three works were, then, historical in focus and scope—with narratives, in fact, encompassing several centuries. And they were historical in the further sense, as well, that the ideals and concepts animating them—for example, individualism and spontaneity for Hayek, human needs and freedom for Polanyi, leadership and rationality for Schumpeter—were fully embedded in a historical narrative, rather than abstracted from a supposedly timeless matrix of ideals.

What would it mean, then, to read Schumpeter's work, in general, as one should read all three of these wartime works? The historicism of Schumpeter's work was rooted in his belief that all social inquiry involved the study of a broad, interrelated process playing out in historical time, rather than the identification of isolated facts or sequences of events, or patterns of uniformity found in notionally separate "historical" cases. It was historical change and historical embeddedness that colored and gave meaning to the facts, concepts and ideals out of which explanation and argument were built. To speak intelligently and comprehensively of "rationality," for example, was to speak not just of a human capacity outside of history, but also (perhaps even more so) to speak of a particular process during a particular period of history, namely "rationalization." More concretely, Schumpeter took it for granted that societies and social formations were complex and tension ridden, and that they rose and fell over time, so that the existing one—the capitalist order, as he called it—could not be expected to last forever. Socialism, from this standpoint, could not adequately be seen just as a set of mistaken ideas (although in a sense it was that for Schumpeter) but was also a likely outcome of certain social tendencies at work in the capitalist order itself.

How Historical Lags Shaped Schumpeter's Influence

It is difficult to imagine those influenced by Hayek forgetting that he thought twentieth-century collectivists had strayed from a path established long ago during the Renaissance, or those influenced by Polanyi forgetting that he saw modern Western history as a centuries-long struggle between the coercive and dislocating process of turning labor and land into commodities and various humane responses. But readers have often abstracted particular ideas of Schumpeter's from their places in a broad narrative of the rise and fall of the capitalist order. Reading Schumpeter properly would entail reading him not just historically but also politically, for Schumpeter's politics were shaped by his sense of history. His political thought, that is, could not adequately be described just in terms of allegiance to particular ideals, but only in terms of a theory of and a response to historical developments.

The point is, of course, that for various reasons—ironically, because of what we could term *historical* reasons—Schumpeter was often not read as I have just suggested he should have been by those who first incorporated his ideas into the main currents of social science. This is where the disjunctures I have mentioned played their part. Some aspects of these disjunctures are more broadly historical and some more personal and biographical.

The first gap is the temporal one between the era in which Schumpeter formulated his main ideas, then eventually wrote and published *Capitalism, Socialism and Democracy*—roughly 1918 to 1942—and the period during which scholars and others began to make use of many of his ideas and arguments, especially the crucial decades of the 1950s and 1960s.[1] Although the difference in years is nowhere near as great, for example, as that between Aristotle and his contemporary readers, it was perhaps more treacherous because most interpreters probably never considered how significant it might be. *Capitalism, Socialism and Democracy* was of course first reviewed shortly after it was published. And these wartime reviews correctly emphasized Schumpeter's historical perspective, his view of liberal capitalism as complex and changing, and especially his projection of trends leading to capitalism's demise. A 1944 review in the *Yale Law Journal*, for example, assessed the book in light of "this age of troubled transition" and focused on Schumpeter's "reluctant obituary" for capitalism (Lans 1944, 830, 842). And of course no one who has read the book fails to see capitalism's doom as an animating theme.

But those who made Schumpeter's ideas canonical did so during an era experienced in the industrialized West as one of economic growth and hegemonic balance—if not exactly stability—a period lasting from the end of Second World War until the early 1970s. I do not underrate the importance of the many momentous events and upheavals of this period, from Chiang Kai-shek's retreat to Taiwan to the Montgomery Bus Boycott and the Battle of Algiers. But recognizing these does not undermine my point: that while the decay or demise of capitalism (indeed upheaval for the whole structure of society) seemed like real possibilities to many in Western Europe and North America in the 1930s and 1940s, the same regions experienced a period of almost unprecedented capitalist prosperity and expansion in the later period. And although it is true that the Soviet Union, in particular, emerged from the war with a powerful military and the ability to impose repressive domestic regimes from Moscow to Prague, in the West it was precisely international communism, rather than domestic socialism, that was seen as the threat—a threat that was perceived largely as force external or at least alien to the liberal capitalist regimes of the world. Indeed the competition between capitalist and communist blocs made obsolescent many of the rivalries that had characterized the "age of catastrophe" and led to World Wars. Thus if the *Road to Serfdom* was a characteristic work of the mid 1940s, Daniel Bell's *The End of Ideology* (1960) could be said to have had the same status a decade-and-a-half later. Bell's view, expressed in that book, was that precisely the ideas and tendencies that seemed so threatening or poignant to the likes of Schumpeter, Hayek, and Polanyi had radically diminished in the West of the 1950s. An age of conflicting social visions and crisis seemed to many intelligent people in the industrialized West to have been replaced by an age of exhausted consensus and stability.[2]

Complicating the problems created between this temporal gap is another more particular to Schumpeter: that lag between the era in which his political allegiances and affinities were first formed and in which he wrote *Capitalism, Socialism and Democracy.* The latter work was surely a response to its time, or to the 1930s and 1940s, but it was in particular the response of someone who valued a much older kind of politics, one that American and English readers in the 1950s and 1960s knew little about—indeed, the response of a conservative groping intellectually for ways to preserve aspects of that sort of traditional politics. Even those who knew Schumpeter at Harvard in the 1940s more often thought of his youth and young adulthood in Central Europe as an explanation for his quaint manners and idiosyncratic persona than for a distinctive political outlook deserving or perhaps even requiring elucidation. Later, and more broadly, it was far easier for scholars who did not recognize or simply could not take seriously some of Schumpeter's allegiances to dismiss the relevance of his sociopolitical outlook in general.

A third disjuncture can be discerned in the culmination of scholarly trends already underway in the 1930s and 1940s: what Robert Dahl could by 1961 term a "successful protest" (Dahl 1961) staged by behavioralist social scientists. A general inclination to study society and politics "scientifically" had existed in American universities since early in the century, but the behavioralist expression of this inclination only became the dominant mode of social science inquiry a decade after Second World War.[3] For our purposes, the most important aspects of this new approach were: the aspiration of its adherents to study simple "behavior"; the view that this could lead to the discovery of general empirical laws of behavior; and a stated insistence on value-free research. By "behavior," scholars of this persuasion meant simple, supposedly unmediated descriptions of things people did, viewed as discrete, irreducible events in the political and social world. Since behavioralists assumed that uncontroversial, value-free descriptions of behavior were possible, they argued that social science was a quest to discover general patterns or correlations among such notionally basic events. But the focus on "behavior" and on general empirical laws along with the type of value-freedom behavioralists sought were inconsistent with Schumpeter's actual historical approach. Like many behavioralists, Dahl (1961, 763, 765) saw the distinction between history and behavioral science simply as one between scholars engaged in mere impressionistic description and others engaged in true causal explanation. But Schumpeter considered history to be a sort of master subject. His historical perspective was focused not on universal empirical laws but on a vision of the transition from one kind of society, with its own tendencies and causal mechanisms, to another form of society, with different ones. From such a standpoint, events were not discrete, irreducible, and atomistic, but connected to each other in and through the continuing process of historical transformation. Moreover, while Schumpeter always was sharply critical of anyone he thought subordinated social-scientific inquiry to partisan or ideological purpose, the behavioralist norm of value neutrality was based on views Schumpeter did not share—that judgments of fact could be permanently and categorically separated from judgments of value, and that "behavior" could be described atheoretically and uncontroversially. Despite these significant differences, those social scientists who rediscovered Schumpeter in the 1950s and 1960s and who subsequently established his reputation in disparate fields often tended to portray him as a behavioral scientist, and in so doing ignored the guiding threads of historical narrative and political interest running throughout his work. Of course, such an interpretation did not flow logically or necessarily from their precepts—it was from any standpoint an error to mistake a prescriptive view of social science for an actual description of a particular social scientist's practice—but it is easy to see how it could have happened, given how hegemonic the behavioral worldview had become in a relatively short time.[4]

The joint effect of these disjunctures was that for many years, the historical narrative or account connecting much of his thought was missed or ignored. And in particular, Schumpeter's idea that what he termed the capitalist order was a particular set of institutions and social relations possessing conflictual, dynamic tendencies and sure to transform into something else was passed over as *obiter dicta* by interpreters in an apparently more stable era, readers who in any case thought in terms of essentially abstract, ahistorical, or nonhistorical categories such as "behavior" and "political systems." In itself, this made it harder to see Schumpeter as a political thinker, since, as I have suggested, the conceptual blocks of his political thought all take on their meaning precisely from a broad historical narrative. But in addition, scholars often simply passed over political commitments that might have seemed unbecoming of a social scientist (as they understood the role) or dramatically out of phase with the postwar world as they understood it. In the decades after his death, then, Schumpeter did have great influence, but primarily that influence was as the creator of a series of relatively distinct theories about discrete subjects.

It may seem that I have focused my explanation so far solely on the reception and influence of *Capitalism, Socialism and Democracy*

(1942), but what I have said largely applies to Schumpeter's sociologically and historically oriented work generally. Partly this is because most of the main arguments and ideas in *Capitalism, Socialism and Democracy* were anticipated in earlier works, such that the later volume can be treated as a sort of compendium of his social, economic, and political ideas and views. And likewise the story of its influence may be taken as representative of Schumpeter's influence generally. More than this, however, the time and the manner in which Schumpeter's various works were read also led to his broadest social and political writings getting much the same treatment as did the 1942 book. We can follow this in three steps. First, for decades, Schumpeter was recognized by many scholars almost exclusively as an economist, the author of *The Theory of Economic Development* (1911) and *Business Cycles* (1939). It was surely on the basis of such work that he was hired and wooed by universities in the 1920s, 1930s, and 1940s. Schumpeter may at times have reinforced this view of himself, for according to Sweezy, he "rarely mentioned his own writings on imperialism and social classes" in his Harvard years, "and it is likely that the vast majority even of the students who came under his direct influence were unfamiliar with this work" (Sweezy 1951, 119). Second, *Capitalism, Socialism and Democracy* did get some notice when it was published, even in countries largely preoccupied with war. But its broad interdisciplinary approach, historicism, and political focus were usually taken (wrongly) as aberrant. One early reviewer thus wrote, "a leading theorist in the field of pure economics, here cuts loose and gathers into the sweep of his analysis psychological, cultural, historical and political considerations which the pure economist is conventionally supposed to shun or to be incapable of handling" (Wolfe 1943, 265). Third, in the 1950s and afterwards, when scholars finally returned to Schumpeter, they approached his body of work, both the sociohistorical essays and even *Capitalism, Socialism and Democracy*, with scalpels, extracting from it discrete concepts and leaving behind the historical and political narrative holding the pieces together. For this reason, more than any other, dividing the remaining discussion of Schumpeter's influence into six separate sections accurately reflects the propagation of his ideas.

Elite Democracy

Because of these disjunctures affecting how Schumpeter was understood by later social theorists, Schumpeter's elite conception of democracy, encapsulated in a simple definition—or at most a few chapters of *Capitalism, Socialism and Democracy*—has frequently been appropriated without reference to the broader conservative historical narrative of Schumpeter's opus. That fate, of course, has not prevented the elite conception of democracy from becoming one of the two most recognized and admired all of his legacies. It influenced key political scientists and sociologists in the 1950s, and their prominent use of the conception turned it into a touchstone for later generations. Today, Schumpeter is nearly as closely associated with elite theories of democracy as, for example, John Locke is with labor theories of property, or Sigmund Freud is with the idea of the unconscious mind.

Yet the earliest reviews of *Capitalism, Socialism and Democracy*, which focused generally on Schumpeter's assessment of the tendencies he thought were leading toward the replacement of capitalism by socialism, treated the elite conception of democracy as a "method" or "institutional arrangement" as just a step in that argument. It was for such readers subsidiary to the argument that there was no incompatibility between socialism and democracy. Moreover, several reviewers were highly critical of the chapters on democracy. The economist Joan Robinson was enthusiastic about the volume in general, concluding: "no matter whether it convinces or not, this book is worth the whole parrot-house of contemporary orthodoxies" (Robinson 1943, 383). But she found the "section on Democracy" to be "perhaps the weakest part of the whole" (382). Another reviewer faulted Schumpeter for making a show of knocking over "the straw man of eighteenth-century rationalism" (Wolfe 1943, 267), but seemed to find little else in the section to comment upon. But this would not continue to be the mainstream judgment for long.

One of the first prominent books to make use of Schumpeter's elite conception of democracy was the seminal 1954 public opinion study, *Voting* (1954). The book's authors, Bernard Berelson, Paul Lazarsfeld, and William McPhee, interviewed voters in the small city of Elmira, New York as they prepared to take part in the presidential election of 1948, and concluded that the formation of political opinions was a group rather than an individual process, one in which ethnic identity, class, and social networks were the important forces. In a concluding chapter, they drew on Schumpeter in arguing that the findings were encouraging, not disquieting, about the prospects of democracy. Resting on Schumpeter's elite conception, they argued that democracy did not require much understanding or participation on the part of average citizens. Although their research suggested that individual voters might not be up to the tasks of rational opinion-formation, democracy of a certain kind could function regardless, they said. Indeed, the lack of interest in politics that attended thin political knowledge and meager participation was probably a good thing, they said, since it allowed elites to forge compromises with the knowledge that citizens would go along. Arguments like this became such a mainstay of political science in the 1950s, 1960s, and 1970s that they served as a new (and negative) focal point for democratic theorists wishing to outline what they saw as a more thorough and "participatory" model of democracy consistent with modern life. Carole Pateman, author of one of the classic statements of the new critique, could complain that by the 1970s "the prevailing academic orthodoxy" was so hegemonic that it had not "been subjected to substantive, rigorous criticism" (Pateman 1970, 103).

Schumpeter's elite conception of democracy had a distinctive, though equally profound, effect on the economist Anthony Downs, one of the progenitors of the rational choice approach to politics. That approach and its cousins, formal theory, public choice theory, and game theory, generally apply models of individual decision-making derived from neoclassical economics to help explain political situations. Use of rational analysis and formal techniques is now so established and widespread that most of those who employ them have likely learned them from mentors who themselves have lost touch with the founding moments of rational choice explanation in political science. But Downs is generally seen as an originator of a theoretical current in rational choice that views the voting decision as a self-interested and calculative one; that conceptualizes political ideologies as points in space (on a left-right axis, classically); and that emphasizes parties as political actors that choose their positions in ideological space in order to win the most support from rational voters. And Downs wrote in *An Economic Theory of Democracy* (1957, 29 n. 11) that it was Schumpeter's elite-centered view of democracy that helped him formulate this approach. What Downs took from Schumpeter, of course, was not a view of voter choice—here Schumpeter and Downs differed substantially—but rather a conception of the centrality and the motivation of political elites. Downs's view of parties as formulating ideologies in order to position themselves for optimal electoral support drew heavily on Schumpeter's claim that politicians used policy positions to win political power through elections, rather than using electoral support to enact policies—or as he put it more provocatively, using the words of an unnamed politician, "What businessmen do not understand is that exactly as they are dealing in oil so I am dealing in votes" (Schumpeter [1942] 1976, 285). Rational choice theory has moved in directions that Schumpeter could scarcely have imagined—indeed, that he would have found wrongheaded. And few contemporary studies using rational choice and related approaches any longer mention Schumpeter. But there was something about the force and clarity of his chapters on democracy as elite competition that opened up political life as a tractable field for an economist. And that has turned out to be epochal to the development of political science.

Most broadly, what Schumpeter bequeathed to later generations of political scientists was a definition of democracy—an attitude toward democracy, certainly, arguments about democracy, to a degree, but most of all a definition. David Ricci was surely on to something, then, when he wrote in the 1980s that behavioralist political scientists, drawing on "voting studies such as that by Berelson, and having Schumpeter's definition of democracy at hand for briefly stating their point . . . discarded the idea that there can be a mandate flowing directly from an informed and alert citizenry up to their government" (Ricci 1984, 162). The Schumpeterian definition so many political scientists drew on was this: democracy was "that institutional arrangement for arriving at political decisions in which individuals acquire the power to decide by means of a competitive struggle for the people's vote" (Schumpeter [1942] 1976, 269). Often it was argued that this definition could be made "operational," meaning that it pointed to readily observable phenomena. But its appeal was not just in its referring to observable phenomena, but in its justifying the application of an honorific term to governments many political scientists frankly liked. "Democracy" according to the definition abstracted from Schumpeter was simply the name for the political arrangements of the United States, Britain, and a few other Western countries in the 1950s and 1960s. This not quite legitimate intermingling of definition-by-characteristic (democracy is defined by quality *x*) with definition-by-example (democracy refers to regimes *a*, *b*, and *c*) may now seem unremarkable to many readers. But it was by no means obvious for many decades before the adoption of Schumpeter's elite conception, that "democracy" would be taken to refer unreservedly to any existing institutions at all. "Democracy," like "justice," might have largely continued to have an aspirational and critical meaning that few would think to conflate with the designation of existing regimes. But only a few political scientists took such an approach—for example, Robert Dahl, who proposed a more neutral term, "polyarchy," to refer to the American and similar polities.

In any case, down to today, Schumpeter's elite conception is accepted as one of the chief available models of democracy—on hand either for sympathetic use or as a foil. Essentially every attempt at an exhaustive account of existing approaches includes Schumpeterian elite theory under one designation or another, often noting, like one scholar, its "extraordinary impact on the development of democratic theory in the aftermath of World War II, especially in the budding disciplines of political science and sociology" (Held 2006, 141).[5]

Innovative Capitalism

I have suggested that in tracing Schumpeter's influence, we have to keep in mind that Schumpeter, the analytical historian, seems at times to have slipped from view. Since no one ever failed to recognize Schumpeter as an economist, reconstructing the influence over time of his most central economic contributions is a distinct task from recounting the influence of his broader social-scientific vision and ideas. And yet intellectual developments in economics that paralleled those in other social sciences—especially a growing emphasis on mathematical models and statistical techniques, with a corollary methodological disdain for history—had a corollary effect on how Schumpeter was read by economists.

The keys to Schumpeter's economic thought, from 1911 onwards, were a theory innovation and a theory of business cycles built upon it. But however impressed with this contribution economists may have been, they have often found it difficult to absorb Schumpeter's work into their own.

Even as early as 1934, when Schumpeter published a revised and translated *Theory of Economic Development*, reviewers portrayed his emphasis on entrepreneurs and innovation as "unconventional" (Howey 1935, 91), a fact that perhaps led them to downplay this aspect of the book. The emphasis was often placed on Schumpeter as offering a set of distinctive theories on well-established problems in economics, such as interest and credit, even though the common element of all those theories, what made them different, was precisely Schumpeter's theory of innovation (Hansen 1936). A few years later, early reviews of *Business Cycles* (1939) were almost uniformly respectful but were also frequently critical—skeptical that Schumpeter had adequately explained why innovations should appear in swarms, for example, and dubious about the way Schumpeter tried to resolve changes in economic outputs over time into three types of cycles of varying duration.[6] And like the reviews of the English edition of the *Theory of Economic Development*, they focused less on innovation itself than on the economic wave-motion Schumpeter thought it engendered. A wartime article by Schumpeter's junior colleague and friend, the Marxist economist Paul Sweezy, may be taken as the exception that proves the rule. True to its title, the article did focus on innovation, per se, but it noted that Schumpeter was by 1943 "known primarily as a business-cycle theorist" and suggested that the preoccupations of "English and American economics" tended to exclude the issues of "change and development" that were central for Schumpeter and the very stuff of his theory of innovation (Sweezy 1943, 93). The tendency to skirt innovation and developmental economics were fully in evidence even in the book edited by Seymour Harris (1951) celebrating Schumpeter's accomplishments just after his death. That volume contained separate essays on the "monetary aspects" of Schumpeter's thought, on his theory of interest, his business cycle theory, and his view of monopoly—but no discrete, separate treatment of the entrepreneur or of innovation.

Behind these treatments of Schumpeter's work—which continued to be characteristic well into the 1970s—were several broader developments in economics. There is, in fact, fairly wide agreement both as to the disappearance of the innovating entrepreneur from the 1930s to the 1980s and as to the basic explanations for it. Perhaps the most discernible of these factors was the increasing mathematization of economics. In the view of one economist writing in the 1960s, it was this general trend—and in particular, the quantifying simplification according to which "the firm is . . . taken to perform a mathematical calculation which yields optimal (i.e., profit maximizing) values for all of its decision variables"—which explains the fact that the entrepreneur "virtually disappeared from the theoretical literature"

(Baumol 1968, 64, 67). The problem, from this standpoint, is that economists generally found themselves unable to incorporate innovation into models constructed according to the dominant approaches: "economic theory has failed to develop an illuminating formal analysis of entrepreneurship" (64). One scholar has argued more pointedly that economists' desire for a certain sort of theoretical tidiness was the key factor. Economists, according to this view, built microeconomics around "a set of internally consistent, nested models, a series of pieces that fit perfectly together to form a grand unified whole" (Barreto 1989, 2). But "any attempt to introduce the entrepreneur into this theoretical structure destroys the internal consistency of the model" (2). A corollary of the increasing mathematization of scholarly economics was a distancing of the field from work in other social sciences, especially from research that employs nonstatistical and nonmathematical methods, such as historical, archival and interpretive work.[7] Despite Schumpeter's attempts to marshal statistics in *Business Cycles*, that book makes it clear how central an historical viewpoint and interpretive, archival research was to his understanding of the study of innovation.[8]

The work of Israel Kirzner (1973) might seem to constitute an exception to all this. Yet Kirzner's theory of the entrepreneur actually underscores much of the foregoing argument, for in sharp contrast to Schumpeter, Kirzner regarded the entrepreneur not as an innovator at all but as a kind of arbitrageur whose activity actually promoted price competition and movement toward equilibrium.

The equilibrium-disrupting Schumpeterian conception of innovation was revived in the 1980s, and continues now to motivate a visible minority of scholars pursuing several different lines of inquiry. The reasons are not entirely certain. Perhaps when the long postwar era of apparently unqualified success at Keynesian economic management seemed to end in the 1970s—with inflation, recession, energy shocks, joblessness, and government deficits haunting the United States and many European countries—Schumpeter's non-Keynesian approach to economics seemed appealing (Sundbo 1998, 4). Or perhaps the shift was simply due to more autonomous scholarly developments. Regardless, one group of scholars often termed "neo-Schumpeterian" focuses on a form of technological competition among business firms suggested by the term "creative destruction," which they argue results in a type of evolution of businesses.[9] Another group of scholars emphasizes that Schumpeter's theory of innovation can only be fully appreciated and developed further with the help of an approach that views entrepreneurship broadly as a form of social leadership, and incorporates history and sociology along with economic theory (Arena and Dangel-Hagnauer 2002). A third approach deeply influenced by Schumpeter may reach a broader audience than the other two because it has been developed within the context of the case-study method employed in many business schools. For example, Thomas McCraw, author of one of the most recent intellectual biographies of Schumpeter, has also edited a collection of essays on business history, focusing on the role of innovative entrepreneurship in disparate economic settings (McCraw 1997). It is a kind of confirmation of Schumpeter's later arguments that innovation could be institutionalized—that it was not just a matter of inexplicable individual genius—that works attempting to teach entrepreneurship have become staples of business school pedagogy.

We are left, then, with a paradox—one that can be viewed from more than one perspective. Simply as an economist, Schumpeter is still almost universally recognized as a "great," to use his own expression for some of his predecessors. But his example is not nearly as frequently followed as it is cited. To some degree, since the education of economists no longer emphasizes the history of the discipline, this is surely true of David Ricardo and John Maynard Keynes, as well. But it seems particularly characteristic of Schumpeter and his intellectual legacy. So we find Robert Heilbroner writing in *The Worldly Philosophers*: "As analyst or visionary, everyone interested in economics must come to grips with him, not only because of what he accomplished within the discipline, but because in his very achievements he demonstrated its limitations" (Heilbroner 1999, 310). And among those particular interested in his theory of innovative capitalism we find a related double response to Schumpeter. He is famous for his theory of innovation—"the innovation theory of the economy is usually attributed to [him]"—but at the same time, innovation theory is itself no more than "a particular school of economic thinking . . . still outside 'mainstream' economics" (Sundbo 1998, 4). Only among what we might term political proponents of free enterprise do we find no trace of this paradox in Schumpeter's influence, but that is a matter for the next chapter.

Tax States

As we have seen, the crux of Schumpeter's argument in his 1918 essay, "The Crisis of the Tax State," was an analysis of the historical development and characteristic tendencies of the modern liberal state, viewed from the standpoint of the interrelation of economics, politics, and war. The modern state or "tax state," he contended, was distinctive in its simultaneous separation from and reliance upon private market activity. Schumpeter argued this state arose out of the fiscal crisis of early modern princes mobilizing large armies, and that its creation and growth had fostered the spread of capitalist rationality. These political and cultural changes also spelled the beginning of the end for feudalism, he claimed. Finally, he had argued that because of the tax state's dependence on market activity, there was a level of taxation beyond which the state could not go without endangering the whole system. When popular demands grew to the point that they could not be met without such levels of taxation, the tax state—and indeed capitalism—would have reached a crisis. This is so rich a story that those who have drawn on it have been able to proceed in several directions.

With "Tax State" we have again a contribution that had significant influence after Schumpeter's death. Little noted during his lifetime by the economists who largely established the parameters of his reputation, it was even left out of what might have been a more comprehensive volume of his contributions in sociology, a 1951 volume with translations of his imperialism and class essays. But "Crisis of the Tax State" was republished in German in 1953 and in English in 1954, and thereafter several times (Augello 1991).

Three analytically separable aspects of "Crisis of the Tax State" proved key to its influence. The first was simply the idea of fiscal sociology itself—the view that "public finances" could provide great insight into "the laws of social being and becoming" and constitute "one of the best starting points for an investigation of society, especially though not exclusively of its political life" (Schumpeter [1918] 1991, 101). The second was Schumpeter's specific conception of the "tax state," a particular sort of modern governmental entity that purported to represent broad public interests but required for its existence the flourishing of private, self-interested activities. And the third was the idea that such state could face a "crisis" if demands on it exceeded the tax revenues it could raise without endangering the economy it depended upon.

The broadest of these influences is simply the idea of "fiscal sociology" itself. Schumpeter himself noted that the Austrian socialist, Rudolf Goldscheid, was "the first to have laid proper stress on this way of looking at fiscal history" (Schumpeter [1918] 1991, 100). But thereafter, most scholars have given credit both to Goldscheid and Schumpeter as seminal contributors. Fiscal sociology has remained a fairly small field—one still in its "infancy" even into the 1990s, according to a proponent (Campbell 1993, 163). It is a much smaller field than the more established domain of "public finance," in whose textbooks "Schumpeter's name rarely appears" (Backhaus 2002, 61). As one scholar puts it: "Professional historians . . . have rarely shared Schumpeter's enthusiasm for the potential for understanding a society through the history of its taxation" (Brownlee 1996, 4). Still, since at least 1975, a range of historically minded scholars, including authors of works on the history of taxation in the West or in Europe generally (Bonney 1999, 6, 13; Hobson 1997, 5–6), American fiscal history particularly (Brownlee 1996, 3–4, 9, 10, 23), and the relationship between state revenues and political development (Braun 1975, 243, 245–6; Sacks 1994, 7), all credit Schumpeter with helping to fashion the conception of fiscal sociology enabling their various contributions. But the recognition is not universal. John Brewer's noted study (1989) of the way in which an efficient taxation system help Britain rise to world power after 1688, for example, does not rest on Schumpeter's work.

"The Crisis of the Tax State" had a somewhat different influence on two opposed but related lines of argument that developed in the 1970s—interestingly, around the same time that economic difficulties in Europe and America were prompting a reexamination of Schumpeter's innovation theory. Proponents of both arguments revived the idea that tax states could face crisis if they were called upon to raise more revenues from the private economy than the private economy could sustain. Yet the uses to which social theorists put this argument differed dramatically.[10] James O'Connor was one of the first to view the problem as one of the competing imperatives facing postwar welfare states, whose citizens demanded that governments meet basic human needs, but which were required, at the same time, to ensure that the capitalist engine functioned well. The problem, according to O'Connor and others, was that citizen demands for protection from market forces could increase to the point that the taxes needed to meet them threatened capitalism. The conflict, so described, pitted political legitimation against economic accumulation. Similar arguments were elaborated by theorists such as Jürgen Habermas (1975) and Claus Offe (1984). O'Connor ([1973] 2004, 3–4) was particularly clear in noting that his argument was "based on the study of fiscal politics," which he traced to Goldscheid and Schumpeter. O'Connor's point was that some alternative to the capitalist tax state—a form of socialism—had to be chosen. While Schumpeter was no socialist, it would be unreasonable to deny that O'Connor's was in fact a distinctively Schumpeterian argument. A very different view of the same dilemma was taken by writers such as Daniel Bell and Samuel Huntington. Bell (1976, 227, 232) both acknowledged O'Connor and referred to Schumpeter's tax-state analysis as "remarkable," "neglected," and "prescient." For him, however, the solution to the dilemma of modern welfare states was a new public philosophy that would mitigate escalating individualistic, almost hedonistic demands on the state. It is an interesting quirk in the history of ideas that Huntington (1975, 73) would in turn cite O'Connor and Bell—not Schumpeter directly—for their analysis of the state's fiscal crisis. Yet his response to the crisis and the view of democracy in which it was embedded clearly also drew on different Schumpeterian arguments which, as we have seen, had entered into the common sense of Anglo-American political science twenty years earlier. What was needed, he said, was a restoration of "governmental authority" to cure "democratic distemper," as well as a recognition that the scope of democratic practices and of participation should be limited (Huntington 1975, 74–113).[11]

By comparison to the ideas of fiscal sociology and the crisis of the tax state, other aspects of Schumpeter's essay never had much influence. As I have pointed out, Schumpeter elaborated in "Tax State" a theory of the transition from feudalism to capitalism. But although this topic has been one of intense episodic interest among historians, Schumpeter's view of the question has not been seriously revived, even though his younger colleague and friend, Paul Sweezy, was a crucial figure in the first round of debates in the 1950s (Sweezy et al. 1976).

Even so it is remarkable that a 1918 essay, aimed at providing some perspective on the problems attending the close of the First World War, eventually anchored a subdiscipline and became a crucial reference for an iconic debate about the acute economic and political problems liberal capitalist democracies faced almost sixty years later.

Atavistic Empires

Sweezy once wrote that Schumpeter really had more than one theory of imperialism, and added wryly that he "could easily have added another theory without actually repudiating much that he had already written" (1951, 123). And I argued in the last chapter that "The Sociology of Imperialisms" is far more equivocal than many interpreters have admitted. Nevertheless, two fairly simple and highly resonant claims from the essay have frequently been recognized by later writers—that imperialist programs have been produced by the interests and ideas of old warrior classes, and that capitalism (by contrast) has intrinsic tendencies toward pacifism. These striking arguments, though they have outlived their original context, have also been much buffeted by later historical events and academic trends.

"The sociology of imperialisms" had auspicious beginnings. It was originally published in "the most prominent social science journal in Germany," on whose editorial board Schumpeter served, alongside Max Weber (Swedberg 1991b, 20, 92). And indeed, Schumpeter's essays on "Imperialism" and "Classes" were "recognized in pre-Hitler Germany as being among the most important works on their respective subjects" (Sweezy 1951, 119).

When they were republished in Germany and the United States in the 1950s, it was, again, to significant notice and acclaim. Two aspects of this second reception are notable. First is the confirmation that the early reviews of the essays provide for the observation that by the 1950s, Schumpeter's integrated approach to the social sciences—in which both historical methods and a sense of history bound many disparate techniques and subjects in an interdisciplinary whole—was already an oddity, viewed with surprise, nostalgia, and occasional misunderstanding. "In a country where many economists consider themselves demeaned when they even admit that they know any sociology," remarked one reviewer, "it is refreshing" to read work "from the pen of an economist who not only knew sociology but contributed to it" (Davis 1951, 465). G. D. H. Cole noted appropriately that although Schumpeter "ranked mainly as an economist," his "approach to the social studies had always a sociological content" and that "his method is throughout historical" (Cole 1952, 177–8).

The other notable aspect of the essay's reintroduction in the 1950s was how deeply geopolitical tensions and ideological anxieties colored reviews. Daniel H. Kruger began his 1955 review essay this way:

> As the "cold war" developed and lines were clearly drawn, the Communists have been beating the propaganda drums incessantly: "Capitalism is imperialistic!" "Capitalism feeds on war and aggression!" "The capitalist countries are war-mongers!" . . . Whenever the Soviet delegate arises to speak in the United Nations, some variant of this theme appears. In numerous articles in *Pravda*, as reported in *The New York Times* in the last few years, the same charges have reappeared in one form or another. (Kruger 1955, 252)

Against this background, Kruger could not contain his enthusiasm to deploy Schumpeter's essay politically, as "the best counter-declaration to the Communist claim" (Kruger 1955, 252). (This ideological bluntness—so at odds with Schumpeter's political suavity—would surely have made the Austrian blush, as might Kruger's emphatic use of punctuation.) Yet Kruger's enthusiasm notwithstanding, David McCord Wright was quite contrarily concerned that Schumpeter's style in both "Imperialisms" and "Classes" did not exhibit sufficient disdain for Marxism. Readers, he worried, might be too "impressed" by "Schumpeter's use of many Marxist expressions" and get a wrong idea of his commitments (Wright 1951, 98). So he counseled others to "compare these essays with my *Economics of a Classless Society* . . . written under Schumpeter's influence and criticism" (98). Ironically, yet another Cold War reading of the essay by Reinhard Bendix complained about Schumpeter's "anti-Marxist polemic" obscuring the "merit" of his analysis (Bendix 1951, 199).

Nearly thirty years later, Wolfgang Mommsen's survey of theories of imperialism, published in German in 1977, still gave pride of place to contributions by figures like Lenin and Schumpeter, and praised Schumpeter's work as "an impressive achievement" and "an important point of departure for many recent interpretations," especially the variety of "socio-economic" theories that attribute imperialism to "particular social structures and combinations of interests arising from the impact of modern capitalism on pre-industrial societies" (Mommsen 1980, 27, 28, 81). Nevertheless, in Mommsen's view the entire debate in which Schumpeter had originally taken part was "largely based on the experience of a particular period of industrial-capitalist development" (66). Thus it was unlikely to remain unaffected by historical developments.

Especially after 1945, trends and upheavals, both economic and political, would continually challenge scholars and others to rethink and reconceptualize imperialism. The Cold War would also raise the profile of a different sort of great-power rivalry than that which had menaced Europe at the turn of the century. The era of decolonization, especially in Africa and Asia, would tend to make Schumpeter's focus on direct military conquest and political domination by foreign powers seem less germane. And later political and cultural developments in former colonies, such as parts of the Middle East, would highlight a wide array of questions about the effects of colonial rule—but strikingly different questions from those that had divided Hilferding from Schumpeter.

Partly in response to these developments, and partly according to the relatively autonomous pathways of intellectual development, the substance of debates about "imperialism" changed, sometimes dramatically.[12] Detailed historical studies of colonialism began to appear in mid-century. Some of them even argued that the Hilferding-Lenin thesis had it backwards: nationalist economic exploitation did not cause but rather followed from the political partitioning of Africa. In this sense, such arguments, though new, did look back to the beginning of the century. But they did not raise Schumpeter's profile. The Vietnam War and similar conflicts revived for some critics aspects of the imperialism debate to which Schumpeter had contributed in 1919, especially assertions that capitalist objectives undergirded military campaigns. But again, precisely the Marxist side of the old debate, and not Schumpeter's argument itself, received renewed attention, whether positive or negative. Meanwhile, in the 1970s and 1980s, dozens of articles and books appeared advancing and criticizing versions of what came to be known as "dependency" and "world-systems theories." What is crucial about these approaches is that the debate surrounding them, unlike the turn-of-the-century one, was not centered on the presence or absence of economic causes for distinctly military phenomena. Dependency theory, associated with figures such as Paul Baran (1957) and André Gunder Frank (1969), held that countries in Latin America, South and East Asia, and Africa remained underdeveloped not because capitalism had failed there, but because of the exploitive nature of these regions' economic relations to the United States and Europe. Similarly, the "world-systems theory" of Immanuel Wallerstein (1974–89) posited a single global economy and a global division of labor unfavorable to the "developing" world. "Imperialism" in this context could refer quite broadly to imbalances in the world economy rather than to conquest and military action, per se. And although one could, perhaps, construct a Schumpeterian answer to these arguments, it would not be based on Schumpeter's "Imperialisms" but perhaps on *Economic Development* or *Business Cycles.*

Finally, even as these approaches were being debated, the earliest contributions to the now extensive literature on "postcolonial" studies appeared, most prominently Edward Said's *Orientalism* ([1978] 2003). Rather than focusing on economics or even politics, narrowly understood, much postcolonial work, following Said, has criticized the whole modern Western relationship and outlook on the rest of the world, arguing that imperialism has pervaded not just overt government actions and propaganda, but also historical, anthropological, and sociological studies. Especially after the postcolonial intervention, it could rightly be argued by the 1990s that "imperialism" could mean many different things to many different people. No longer just a term for a type of military expansion, as it had essentially been for Schumpeter, it could refer to a seemingly stable world economic regime, to cultural phenomena, or indeed to a comprehensive system of political, economic, and cultural domination. And a closely related shift in the relevant discourses—a very sharp contrast between Schumpeter's and the later scholarship just reviewed—becomes obvious so soon as we note the lack of a sustained discussion in Schumpeter's essay of the parts played by non-European peoples in shaping modern imperialism, as well as its effects on them.[13]

Nearly two decades of related scholarship on "globalization" has not fostered a restoration the terms of debate, circa 1919, nor has the renewed use of terms such as "imperialism" and "empire" to refer to contemporary US power and foreign policy, whether critically (Johnson 2000) or approvingly (Ferguson 2003). Niall Ferguson, for example, has written a widely popular appreciation of British imperial rule and a call to the United States to emulate aspects of it, but he does not refer to Schumpeter's theory of imperialism. Indeed, in its celebration of empire, Ferguson's book is very far in spirit from Schumpeter. And yet, for all the changes since he wrote it, Schumpeter's contribution has remained a distant though notable landmark. Those who write histories and typologies of imperialism theories still often pay their respects to his arguments. A contemporary scholar notes how recent explorations of Japanese imperialism use Schumpeter's concept of atavism, and classifies Schumpeter as someone with lasting influence in the field (Bush 2006, 49, 111). His classic essay, moreover, has again been excerpted in one of the most recent anthologies of imperialism theories (Chilcote 2000). And even scholars who bypass Schumpeter in their assessments of imperialism theories continue to feel the need to explain the omission (Wolfe 1997, 391 n. 11).

Functional Classes

Like "Imperialisms," Schumpeter's essay on "Social classes" was originally published in the most prominent German social science journal, and enjoyed a considerable reputation at the time. But while the subject of imperialism has been a perennial one for almost a century, class has remained far more than that: an almost constant and unavoidable topic for many social scientists.

"Probably more has been written about class than about any other topic in sociology," according to one author of an overview of the topic (Edgell 1993, viii–ix). In the midst of this vast and contentious literature, Schumpeter's theory of class was always less recognized than his theory of imperialism, and the dissipation of that influence in the wake of relevant historical and intellectual trends has been pronounced. Even when "Social classes" was translated and republished just after Schumpeter's death, reviewers were markedly ambivalent. Sweezy, who spearheaded its republication, saw the essay's value less as a stand-alone and transhistorical theory of class formation than as a history of the rise of capitalism, viewed as entailing both the emergence of the bourgeoisie and the decay of the feudal nobility (1951, 120–1). Bendix, who just two years later would include a passage from "Social classes" in the popular anthology on social stratification he published with Lipset, nevertheless found the essay much "weaker" than "Imperialisms."

A number of features of "Classes" probably explain the lack of enthusiasm among later students of class for drawing upon Schumpeter's theory that class hierarchy was due to the superior ability of a class to fulfill a socially useful function. Schumpeter's ambition to devise a theory of class that would not merely explain the features and mechanisms of contemporary social structure but identify the key collective agents and forces driving sociohistorical change has rarely attracted positive attention, except perhaps from Sweezy. In addition, while Schumpeter was confident that social classes were really existing entities or organisms that thought and acted, many later social scientists (but not all) have viewed class mainly as a descriptive category, or a characteristic of individuals. Schumpeter was also convinced that just a few classes, especially nobility, bourgeoisie, and working class, were the key collective actors in the modern world, but many recent social scientists have tended to view even class structure itself as much complicated by gradations of skill, education, and status, and by such trends as the growth of service employment, making Schumpeter's categories appear too imprecise. Relatedly, even the very title of Schumpeter's essay bracketed ethnicity, suggesting that class was the most salient form of collective identity or action, while social science since his time has generally acknowledged the explanatory significance not only of ethnicity, but also of race, gender, and sexual orientation, alongside class. Finally, those since Schumpeter's time who continued to focus on class, per se, have often thought it necessary to chronicle the political and cultural developments that have led to class formation.[14] Indeed, the general view that classes, ethnicities, and racial groups exist only in virtue of complex cultural, social, and political processes, is now a commonplace. But such an outlook finds no corollary in Schumpeter's understanding, despite his recognition of the issue of class "consciousness."

For these and perhaps other reasons as well, one could find few or only peripheral references to Schumpeter's theory of class just a decade or two after his death. Tom Bottomore wrote in his book on Schumpeter's economic sociology that "it is greatly to be regretted that Schumpeter did not pursue this study of social classes" (Bottomore 1992, 54). But, ironically, his own earlier full-length study of class (1966) had made no mention of Schumpeter. In his influential study of *The Class Structure of the Advanced Societies*, the prominent sociological theorist Anthony Giddens mentioned Schumpeter's "famous" and "compelling" idea that classes may be seen as "conveyances" whose shape may not change even though there is turnover of passengers (Giddens 1973, 107).[15] But this was Giddens's only reference to Schumpeter in the book—he did not review the substance of Schumpeter's theory of class—and even this passage he singled out only for criticism. And a great many representative anthologies on class today, covering a variety of viewpoints, simply do not refer to Schumpeter.[16]

Economic Sociology

During the past two decades, a number of scholars have reexamined Schumpeter's work for what it has to say about a subject matter and an approach that can be summed up under the label of "economic sociology." I have already referred to Schumpeter's economic sociology in discussing his doubts about equilibrium understandings of the economy, his conception of the capitalist order, or well as the influence of his theories of the tax state, imperialism, and class. What is at issue for scholars interested in "economic sociology," distinct from such concrete problems as imperialism, is questions about the scope, method, and purpose of social science. As opposed to much of the literature I have discussed in this chapter, the relatively recent works viewing Schumpeter as an economic sociologist do a superb job at reintegrating his influential concepts and arguments into a comprehensible whole. That is, unlike the many social scientists since Schumpeter's death who have plucked this or that idea out of context from his total vision, those interested in economic sociology have found it necessary to show precisely how these different ideas are interrelated. Yet insofar as the principle uniting Schumpeter's writings is seen to be methodological, these works are, ironically, of only secondary interest in a book focused on Schumpeter's political thought. So I shall deal with economic sociology relatively briefly here.

The argument for "economic sociology" can be understood partly as a critique of the approach to economics that stresses only systems of interrelated economic quantities (prices, wages, unemployment rates, gross national production) or agents conceived primarily as followers of behavior rules. As we have seen, for Schumpeter, the problem was not that such economic work was wrong but that it was more limited than its advocates have realized. As Schumpeter put it, "economic analysis"—this limited form of economics—"deals with the questions how people behave at any time and what the economic effects are they produce by so behaving" while "economic sociology deals with the question how they came to behave as they do" ([1954] 1994, 21). For Schumpeter, it was clear that one could not profitably limit oneself to questions such as how consumer behavior influences prices without ever taking up questions such as how social, cultural, and institutional developments produced the very consumer we now take for granted. Economic sociology, he said, could also be seen to involve the "interpretive description" of "economically relevant institutions, including habits and all forms of behavior in general, such as government, property, private enterprise, customary or 'rational' behavior" (Schumpeter [1949] 1989, 293). These two definitions of economic sociology, one gesturing toward the interpretation of institutions and practices and the other toward the analysis of transforming historical change, coincided for Schumpeter because institutions and practices were always transforming—something that could never be captured in an economics that focused on a few simple behavior rules abstracted from both time and from social life and treated, for analytic purposes, as eternal. Schumpeter argued early in his *History of Economic Analysis*: "social phenomena constitute a unique process in historic time, and incessant and irreversible change is their most obvious characteristic" ([1954] 1994, 435). This way of putting the matter combines two ideas: a historical vantage point from which all social phenomena can be seen as interrelated, and recognition that time or duration is a necessary feature of this viewpoint. So Schumpeter stressed here both the artificiality of distinguishing economics and sociology—the idea of "economic sociology" being the child of this revelation—and the idea that the study of historical development is a kind of master subject into which all social-scientific analyses could be fit.

As early as the 1940s and 1950s Sweezy's appreciation of Schumpeter was largely premised on an appreciation of the two sides of "economic sociology" mentioned above. Sweezy argued against seeing essays like "Imperialisms" and "Social classes" as external to his economic thought, and wrote that Schumpeter could be seen as providing a "complete theory of capitalism" consisting of "the theory of origins, the theory of functioning and growth, and the theory of decline" (Sweezy 1951, 121). But as I have already suggested, such a historical and interdisciplinary viewpoint—not to mention the underlying view Sweezy believed he shared with Schumpeter that "capitalism is, like all social systems, a transitory phenomenon" (121)—went against the grain of much social science from the 1950s through the 1970s.

It was only in the late 1980s that, largely as a reaction to the dominant tendencies in social science, economists, sociologists, and others began to turn to Schumpeter precisely for economic sociology. Richard Swedberg has written about the way that Schumpeter's ideas on economic sociology arose out of methodological battles at the turn of the century, especially the so-called Battle of Methods pitting neoclassical economists against more historically minded foes (Swedberg 1989). He argues that Schumpeter's own economic sociology was mainly focused on economic institutions, but suggests that rather than separate camps of mainstream economists working on one set of problems and economic sociologist working on another, a problem-driven approach would be better in which scholars chose the method or approach that best suited the issue at hand (515, 520–1). While agreeing about the formative importance of the "Battle of Methods," Tom Bottomore has emphasized that Schumpeter's deep interest in "processes of economic and social development" created strong affinities and engagement with Karl Marx (Bottomore 1992, 3). Bottomore's ultimate criterion for the value of an approach to social analysis is its ability to explain the leading problems and controversies of the day. Viewing Schumpeter, Weber, and Marx as the main protagonists in any narrative of economic sociology, Bottomore argues that all three wrote at a time when it still seemed possible to structure social science around the ideal-typical forms of capitalism and socialism. But with Soviet communism discredited and discarded, with successful capitalism almost everywhere accompanied by active welfare states, and with new problems, especially environmental ones, looming on the horizon, economic sociology today must be flexibly responsive to different practical challenges (Ch. 8). Yuichi Shionoya (1997) places Schumpeter's economic sociology alongside several related features of his thought, including his approach to economic development, the history of economic thought, and the issue of science and ideology. Although to some degree specialized themselves, these authors are a superb resource for those interested in Schumpeter, providing an analytically coherent yet inclusive view of Schumpeter's contributions in social science that contrasts with many of the narrower treatments of Schumpeter's ideas that characterized his legacy for forty years.

* * *

Since I have devoted considerable attention to the way a variety of academic disciplines and subdisciplines have changed so as to reduce, in some cases, the influence of Schumpeter's contributions, it may seem that I believe Schumpeter's intellectual influence is no longer significant. But assessments of scholars' influence too often exaggerate by limiting the record to those few descendants who most praise the figure in question. There is more to be learned from realistically charting the change of disciplines over time and the effect of these changes on notable concepts and arguments. And a skeptical and wide-ranging survey demonstrates far more reliably than selective quotation could the impressive staying-power of many of Schumpeter's vivid theories and concepts, even in the face of the profound shocks and transformations of the twentieth century. After many waves of democratization from Latin America to the former Soviet republics—and many surges of democratic disillusionment as well—Schumpeter's definition of democracy is still widely used by scholars, for better or worse. Although the colonial struggles that first precipitated debates about "imperialism" have long since receded from the political imaginary, and the term has come to be applied to quite disparate phenomena and relations, Schumpeter's linking of foreign domination to atavistic social relations still demands recognition today. More broadly, even after accounting for great changes in each of the relevant fields to which Schumpeter contributed, we can see that he persists as a touchstone and sometimes even as figure whose ideas shape ongoing research and writing. And that is something that we can honestly say about few intellectuals more than 120 years after their births.

4

Relevance

In a comically surreal scene of the film *Annie Hall*, the title character's boyfriend, played by Woody Allen, grows increasingly vexed with a know-it-all professor in line behind them at the cinema, a man who has been discoursing for several minutes on the film director Federico Fellini, the playwright Samuel Beckett, and the media theorist Marshall McLuhan. Finally unable to contain himself, Allen steps out of his role (and out of cinematic realism) to find McLuhan himself behind a movie signboard. "I heard what you were saying," McLuhan obligingly tells the offending academic. "You know nothing of my work." Speaking directly to the camera, Allen muses, "Boy, if life were only like this." Indeed. If it were only so uncomplicated and so gratifying to summon canonical thinkers and use them for our purposes. If only they would appear simply to confirm our interpretations of them, and dutifully to take our sides in contemporary debates. But it does not work this way—and not only when (or because) they are dead.

This is a general problem, of course, whenever we make use of past thinkers for any contemporary purpose. But Schumpeter is, for a variety of reasons, an unusually porcupine-like figure, one who seems deliberately to resist contemporary embrace. In the two main sections of this final chapter assessing the contemporary relevance of Schumpeter's work, I want to look at some of the problems that attend the contemporary appropriations of the Austrian's work. I focus particularly on the use of Schumpeter's work on democracy by contemporary political scientists, and on the appropriation of Schumpeter's opus by conservatives of different varieties, in both cases highlighting Schumpeterian arguments, concepts, commitments, and poses that seem to exceed what different contemporary appropriators might like or can effectively use, given their current challenges or purposes.

Democratic Theory Appropriations

In a section of the previous chapter, I reviewed Schumpeter's influence on political scientists since his death in 1950. I pointed out that some early, seminal works in postwar political science, such as Berelson et al.'s *Voting* and Downs's *Economic Theory of Democracy*, made use of Schumpeter's elite conception of democracy as method. And since then, Schumpeter's method-centered definition of democracy has seemed almost encoded into the DNA of the discipline. The argument of the previous chapter as a whole was that a series of "lags" between the time that Schumpeter wrote and the time he was read or began truly to work his influence on many social scientists accounts for the particular way that his work was influential. In particular, I argued that these lags resulted in Schumpeter's being read less as a conservative with a multifaceted but integrated historical theory of capitalist development, than as the originator of a set of isolated concepts or hypotheses. This section traces the same route in reverse. For beginning with the theory of democracy as method abstracted for use by political scientists, I find the unavoidable surpluses that accompany it, both signs or aspects of Schumpeter's particular conservative narrative of social development.

Overwhelmingly, what political scientists have appropriated from Joseph Schumpeter is his definition of democracy: a minimal one, centered on the existence of electoral institutions sufficient to ensure that those who control the government and therefore make authoritative decisions get that power by winning a competition for votes. And I would suggest that the all-but-unavoidable surplus accompanying that definition is simply Schumpeter's rearguard conservatism. Most of the political scientists who have wanted to appropriate Schumpeter's definition of democracy have accepted a model of social science that centers on value-neutral fact-collection. And many of these political scientists have quite illicitly allowed their desire to practice and promote this sort of social science to blind them to the actual political commitments of the man whose definition of democracy they have wanted to deploy. A more conscientious and aware political scientist might, it is true, wish to argue that despite Schumpeter's conservatism, one could still appropriate the elite competitive definition of democracy without appropriating, for example, the Austrian's deeply rooted appreciation of aristocratic political leadership.

But the elements of Schumpeter's thought are simply not so separable as this implies. Contemporary political scientists may not have to answer, in the first instance, for Schumpeter's appreciation of semifeudal political leadership, but they should be able to provide a truly compelling justificatory account of the definitions they use. As I have pointed out, establishing neutral grounds for particular criteria for democracy is, to say the least, complicated by the fact that the term is never deployed neutrally, but is almost always bestowed as a marker of approval. Given that democracy, as concept, aspiration and practice, has a rather diverse 2,500 year history, what warrant have students of politics for the notably present-centered assumption that the institutions a handful of imperfect Western countries have had for little more than a century constitute the one and true incarnation? The response that the definition of democracy should center on elite competition for votes because elite competition for votes characterizes the politics of those countries that some analysts contend are democratic is drearily uninformative, if not simply circular. Beyond reliance on this, however, few of the social scientists who use Schumpeter's definition have much of an answer, except to rely additionally on Schumpeter's authority. Yet Schumpeter had a cogent answer to this question, probably the most elegant justification that has been offered for his definition of democracy. His argument was that democracy could mean nothing else because most people lack the "individual volition" (or "definite will") that could make any more demanding practice of democracy work. The crucial chapter setting the stage for Schumpeter's redefinition of democracy, we recall, contained a profoundly pessimistic assessment of the political capacities of ordinary people. According to Schumpeter, it was the average citizen's "reduced sense of reality" about politics that led to an "absence of effective volition" (Schumpeter [1942] 1976, 261). The ordinary person's pet "phrases," their "wishes and daydreams and grumbles," and their "likes and dislikes" simply did not, in Schumpeter's estimation, "amount to what we call a will" (261). And the quality of thinking about public affairs was worse than in day-to-day matters. "The typical citizen drops down to a lower level of mental performance as soon as he enters the political field. He argues and analyzes in a way which he would readily recognize as infantile within the sphere of his real interests. He becomes a primitive again" (262).

If one accepts these assumptions, however, it is difficult to understand why one would place much value on democracy at all, even on the minimalist sort Schumpeter proposed. Since, according to Schumpeter's argument, even the occasional act of voting was virtually devoid of reasoned meaning, it was not clear why one would want to construct a political system around it. Schumpeter would likely have responded that minimal democracy was merely a necessary, pragmatic concession to a powerful historical tendency. But most contemporary political scientists likely do not want to be associated with either this dark assessment of human nature or with the view that democracy is just an unpleasant reality of modern social development. And they should be troubled by the fact that, according to the assumptions underlying the definition of democracy they have adopted, the typical person's political life was just "an indeterminate bundle of vague impulses loosely playing about given slogans and mistaken impressions" (Schumpeter [1942] 1976, 253). For if this is so, such a person's democratic rights—voting, association, assembly, and expression—cannot be assigned much value. Schumpeter himself asked, given how little there was to commend the ordinary citizen's "volitions" why anyone should "worship at their shrine, still less why we should feel bound to count each of them for one and none of them for more than one" (259).

And such gloomy assumptions about ordinary agency, of course, were also, in a sense, the indispensable corollary of Schumpeter's conservative understanding of political leadership. While ordinary individuals were barely able to buy shoes without succumbing to irrational impulses, members of political elites, in Schumpeter's view, were defined by an almost preternatural ability to move hundreds or even millions of others to concerted action. In Schumpeter's telling, for example, no sooner had the nineteenth-century British Prime Minister Benjamin Disraeli produced the "spectacular success of the Congress of Berlin"[1] than his rival, William Gladstone "suddenly roused the country by a series of addresses of unsurpassable force . . . which played up the Turkish atrocities so successfully as to place him on a crest of a wave of popular enthusiasm *for him personally*"—a task carried out "single-handed" at that (Schumpeter [1942] 1976, 275–6). Although this is rarely, if ever, acknowledged, such comments, integral to the famous chapters on democracy, are of course also closely connected to Schumpeter's "Tory democracy" memos and to his analysis of the feudal bulwarks of capitalism.

There is also what could be termed an unrecognized methodological surplus for those political scientists who have appropriated Schumpeter's elite conception of democracy. For, like Anthony Downs, they have generally adopted that definition to support a vision of democracy as a stable, self-sufficient political system of mutually influencing parts, especially vote-seeking elite politicians and largely passive voters. But it is quite clear that Schumpeter believed there were limits to such models in general and to this model of democracy in particular—limits rarely if ever acknowledged by Schumpeter's political science followers. One of Schumpeter's important legacies is his economic sociology, itself built upon the idea that standard economic models of the economy were adequate for limited questions of "how people behave at any time" and the "effects" produced by this behavior, but that social science had to be concerned as well with frankly more momentous questions concerning the past and future development of present behavior and institutions (Schumpeter [1954] 1994, 21). The same could be said of contemporary models of political (as opposed to economic) behavior and development. The actors whose characteristic behaviors and relations are often taken for granted in such models actually change in historical time, and an ambitious social science would have to meet the challenge of understanding that causes, direction, and key features of that change. Schumpeter's elite definition of democracy helped him establish his claim that something that could legitimately be termed democracy could exist in tandem with the form of socialism he foretold. But it is quite clear that this was just a single aspect of his overall assessment of the trajectory of Western polities, which assessment itself required an approach or method recognizing societies as complex and (more crucially) tension-ridden wholes, characterized by dynamic tendencies, and constantly on the way to becoming something different from what they presently are.[2] Such an approach to social science offers far more of a rebuke than a confirmation to the practices of the political scientists who have borrowed Schumpeter's elite conception of democracy.

Conservative Appropriations

The interesting question with which we begin examining the impediments to conservative appropriations of Schumpeter is this: If Schumpeter is influential (as he has been) and if he was a conservative (as he was), why has he not been more influential as a conservative, or for conservatives of various kinds? Consider: there is today no Schumpeterian school of contemporary conservatism, as there are Burkean or Straussian schools, nor has Schumpeter been drawn upon heavily by many of the most prominent conservative thinkers and public intellectuals who have written since his death. Perhaps it is no surprise that Leo Strauss, the German emigré whose writings focused on the long historical sweep of Western political philosophy, and who treated much modern social science with suspicion, had little use for Schumpeter. But what of Hayek, a fellow Austrian, social scientist, and defender of capitalism, whom we might expect to have engaged with Schumpeter? In *The Constitution of Liberty*, written nine years after Schumpeter's death, Hayek mentions him only in footnotes. And Schumpeter is again largely (though not entirely) out of sight in Hayek's *Law, Legislation and Liberty* (1973–9). Or again, the fact that Russell Kirk seems to have had no room for thoughts of Schumpeter in *The Conservative Mind* may perhaps be attributed to his Burkean understanding of conservatism's project. But it is notable that Thomas Sowell, an economist by training and one clearly familiar with Schumpeter, has used him mainly as a respected source on the history of economic thought.[3] And it is clear, as well, that in a variety of contemporary journals with varying conservative editorial perspectives, Schumpeter is cited less often than figures from Burke to Hayek, Rand, Strauss, and Milton Friedman.[4] This is of course not to suggest that Schumpeter is unrecognized or unappreciated today. Indeed, there is little question that Schumpeter remains an iconic figure, an established and known point of reference. In 1999, one prominent conservative journal placed *Capitalism, Socialism and Democracy* 13th on its list of "The 100 best non-fiction books of the century" (Miller 1999)—just after Oakeshott's *Rationalism in Politics*.

Schumpeter's reputation as a conservative, however, is fairly narrowly established, founded, more than anything else, on his theory of innovation in capitalism. "There aren't many concepts as beloved by conservatives as the great economist Joseph Schumpeter's notion of creative destruction," write two prominent conservative public intellectuals (Kristol and Brooks 2000, 24). The preponderance of references to Schumpeter in a variety of conservative journals cite innovation or creative destruction—and not, for example, Schumpeter's view of traditional elites. The sometimes extraordinary attention paid to Schumpeter by business magazines and business writers during the last quarter-century has the same focal point. In 1983, the centenary of Schumpeter's and Keynes's births, the renowned management expert Peter F. Drucker was afforded a prominent spread in *Forbes* magazine that concluded: "No one in the interwar years was more brilliant, more clever than Keynes. Schumpeter, by contrast, appeared pedestrian—but he had wisdom. Cleverness carries the day. But wisdom endureth" (Drucker 1983, 128). More recently, *Business Week* accorded similar treatment to Schumpeter (Whalen 2000).[5]

We may begin exploring the way in which Schumpeter seems to resist contemporary appropriation by looking more closely at this most popular Schumpeterian concept, innovation. For even those champions of private enterprise who understandably have been inspired by Schumpeter's theories of creative destruction and innovation face a difficulty. Recall that Schumpeter ultimately stressed innovation, a process or social phenomenon, rather than entrepreneurs, physical or moral persons. What was needed to stimulate economic development, according to his theory, was new productive "combinations," that is, new products and new ways of making, marketing, and delivering them. How these things were introduced, and by whom they were introduced, did not necessarily matter. Schumpeter, of course, preferred that innovations be supplied by entrepreneurs. This was, after all, the key to capitalism's robustness, he thought. For as long as entrepreneurs played this role in society there would be people, indeed a whole powerful class, with a vital stake in defending capitalism. But by the time he wrote *Capitalism, Socialism and Democracy*, he was convinced that it was important to distinguish the phenomenon of innovation from the person of the entrepreneur, and to reckon with the fact that the phenomenon could occur without an inspired individual directing it. As he put it, technological advancement was increasingly carried out by "teams of trained specialists" who proposed, planned, tested new ideas, replacing the entrepreneur's "flash of genius," much to the detriment of the "romance" of "commercial adventure" (Schumpeter [1942] 1976, 132). In fact, we have seen that it is impossible to understand Schumpeter's arguments about capitalist development and the possibility of socialism without recognizing that he thought corporate bureaucracies could provide innovations as well as individual entrepreneurs. Schumpeter even argued that government-controlled socialist enterprise could probably produce technological progress of some sort. The issue is less Schumpeter's view that socialism was imminent than it is the possibility that innovation could take place without the living, breathing figure of the entrepreneur. For economic innovation that is not tied directly to the individual entrepreneur is a remarkably portable concept—one potentially consonant not only with support for unrestricted private enterprise but also with arguments for various sorts of welfare capitalism or even market socialism.

This mutable quality of Schumpeter's innovation argument, then, points toward a broader topic: the Austrian's lack of support for certain prominent themes or tendencies in contemporary conservative discourses. Now, I argued in Chapter 2 that conservatism cannot be defined by any single unanimously shared doctrine, let alone pinned to an entire fixed list of common principles.[6] At best, one can argue that "conservatism" (like other similar labels) refers to shifting ensembles of arguments, values, and assumptions, none of them necessarily shared by all to whom the label "conservative" may be aptly applied. It is for this reason that we need such modifying expressions as "Burkean," "Straussian," "economic libertarian," and so on. And it is for this reason that Hayekians, for example, may have significant differences with neoconservatives, or religious conservatives with followers of Rand.

But it is not at all inconsistent with recognition of this diversity and tension within conservatism to acknowledge, as well, that during certain eras, particular themes and arguments have been especially prominent in conservative public discourses. The ongoing global march of capitalism, the continued importance of religious groups within many conservative movements around the world, and the constantly evolving division of international politics into great powers and lesser ones, have all tended to highlight the significance of at least three quite different recurrent themes. These include economic libertarianism, religious traditionalism, and various arguments for the self-assured use of power by leading liberal capitalist countries. "Economic libertarianism," designates any of a number of arguments advocating limits on public or state intervention in the private economy on the premise that private enterprise embodies or promotes freedom. There are several such arguments, and they are, in principle at least, among the most attractive upon which advocacy of private enterprise may be premised. While not theirs exclusively, such arguments have been put forward with special energy by such economic libertarians as Hayek and Friedman. Religious traditionalism may refer to any of a variety of arguments that seek to root social, economic, or political positions in established religious principles. For example, the official social and political teachings of the Catholic Church have changed considerably since the nineteenth century, when it was a pillar of reaction, but it is still quite correct to view the current Pope, Benedict XVI, as a prominent religious conservative. And conservative religious movements and parties of varying faiths and descriptions continue to play important roles in Europe, the United States, and the developing world. Finally, military and diplomatic assertiveness to promote conservative aims has been a recurrent, though not universal, theme ever since Burke laid out justifications for war against revolutionary France. Contemporary neoconservatism, although it comprises a range of domestic and international arguments, has become known most of all for the view that powerful liberal capitalist democracies should use their dominant positions to advance their interests, defined broadly.

But however prominent they may be in public discourse today, these three heterogeneous themes are of interest in this book, ironically, because Schumpeter's work did not advance them. And this tells us something significant about his current stature. First, then, Schumpeter was not an economic libertarian in the ordinary sense. Certainly Schumpeter saw many virtues in markets, understood realistically, and he could have made common cause with economic libertarians against extensive government intervention and regulation of the private economy. But he did not believe that markets and free enterprise were embodiments or expressions of individual liberty for most participants. And this is chiefly because his most basic assumptions provide no plausible support for such a claim. Schumpeter thought consumer behavior, rather than a free expression of uncoerced, spontaneous desires, was often tradition-bound, on the one hand, and manipulated by marketing and advertising, on the other. Moreover, he did not regard most people as possessing the requisite traits to choose freely. The doubts he raised about rationality in economic theory were in themselves sufficient to raise questions about the capacity for free choice. But we have seen that the underpinnings of his elite democratic theory went much further, calling into question whether the average citizen had either the information or the will-forming capacity necessary to participate meaningfully in politics.

Schumpeter was also not a proponent of liberal capitalist nations building dominant militaries and using them to assert their broadest interests. He was certainly concerned nine decades ago to deny a particular critical unmasking of military campaigns—to argue against the chief Marxist theory of imperialism, holding that a certain phase of capitalism intrinsically and inevitably produced incentives for military expansion. But in so doing in 1918–19, he was not attempting to justify the military postures of any participants in the war, on either side. His argument did not even deny that these countries' policies were imperialistic, but only contested the cause of the imperialism. And stepping back from First World War itself, Schumpeter never flatly denied that it could sometimes be rational for a capitalist country to pursue military adventures for economic reasons; given certain conditions, he thought it could be rational (see Chapter 2). More generally, his writings contain no suggestion at all that he thought a forceful military posture was a proper means of pursuing any valuable political goal. In fact, the evidence suggests that Schumpeter was deeply dismayed by First World War, which he termed a "murderous insanity" even while it raged (Schumpeter [1918] 1991, 119). Rather than providing principled reasons for war or other kinds of force projection, Schumpeter's whole approach was to uncover militarism's atavistic origins. Now, this is not to suggest that Schumpeter "would have" opposed any particular late twentieth or early twenty-first-century war—no one can know—but only that his extant writings provide little support for proponents of projecting power expansively. And to this problem, it is possible to add a rather different and more troubling one. The varied arguments for an assertive military posture have often rested on the need to vigorously check other existing or potential military powers. In the late twentieth century, the iconic example of a power that had to be countered, indeed defeated, has usually been Nazi Germany. Yet as we have seen, Schumpeter himself favored making concessions to Hitler, even after the annexation of Austria, the Munich crisis, and the subsequent invasions of Czechoslovakia and Poland (Allen 1991, 2: 93).[7]

Finally, Schumpeter was not a religious traditionalist in a sense that is likely to be serviceable to contemporary conservatives of that description. He did argue in his Tory democracy memos that high aristocrats should make common cause with church officials as well as appeal to Catholic religious sentiments in constructing a conservative party. But the terms of that argument were frankly instrumental. The goal was to preserve the Austro-Hungarian monarchy by harnessing a segment of the voting population. The memos, then, were devoted explicitly to keeping Austria-Hungary *kaiserlich-königlich* (imperial-royal) rather than to ensuring the sanctity of *Kinder, Küche, Kirche* (children, kitchen, church). For the most part, Schumpeter did not champion what are sometimes now termed "traditional values," nor did he set out to turn back the tide of secularism, or to refute moral relativism. His deepest original commitments were to quite concrete traditional social relations that are no longer often defended, such as monarchy and aristocracy. More recent conservatives sometimes cite Schumpeter's deploring of the falling birthrate, which he considered to be intimately connected with the decay of the bourgeois family. In this context, Schumpeter supported the Catholic Church's opposition to contraception (Schumpeter [1941] 1991, 379). Much of his discussion of the birthrate, however, focused on strictly economic consequences. And when he turned to what might be termed moral issues, the main thrust of his argument was that childlessness undermined many of the motivations promoting hard work and entrepreneurship, including the willingness to fight "tooth and nail" against "taxation, labor unions, and so on" (378). Moreover, Schumpeter voiced sympathetically what he termed a "eugenic doubt," an argument holding that after the deterioration of mores supporting childbearing by the upper classes—those "men and women who want to do something in this life"—"weak-minded mothers" still continued to reproduce at high rates (377). Few of today's religious traditionalists would sympathize. A 1945 address in which Schumpeter spoke favorably about Pope Pius XI's encyclical, *Quadragesimo Anno* might seem to mark him as religious traditionalist. But in it Schumpeter mentioned no intrinsically religious ideas, and he disavowed any desire to "praise a moral message of the Pope," attempting instead to derive from the encyclical a strictly "economic doctrine," the "corporate principle," one closely related not just to Pius, but to policies of Austrian Christian Socials of earlier decades (Schumpeter [1945] 1991, 404).

In addition to these dissonances, aspects of what I have termed throughout this book Schumpeter's "rearguard" political outlook may also pose problems for those who might wish to draw on his work. Almost everyone who knows Schumpeter's work knows he thought capitalism was very likely to be succeeded by socialism. But not as many are familiar with this related understanding of conservatism, already quoted: "[N]o more can be achieved by individual or group volitions than to perform transitions with a minimum of loss of human values. The latter, the bringing about of transitions from your social structure to other social structures with a minimum loss of human values, that is how I should define conservatism" (Schumpeter [1941] 1991, 399). Such a limited, late Habsburg view of what political action can accomplish was not embraced by certain staunch and activist thinkers such as Burke, Hayek, or Friedman, who deplored political and economic trends around them—key figures who are all more frequently cited than Schumpeter in contemporary conservative discourses.

The distinctiveness of Schumpeter's rearguard attitude can be demonstrated with reference to a well-known argument by Albert O. Hirschman. In *The Rhetoric of Reaction*, Hirschman contends that conservatives, in arguing against "progressives" and revolutionaries of various kinds, have developed three types of "theses," including the "futility thesis," which holds that "attempts at social transformation will be unavailing" (Hirschman 1991, 7). The gist of the "futility thesis" is that those who attempt dramatically to reform social and political institutions will fail because of the inviolability of social laws or the resistance of traditional social structures. Whether or not we accept Hirschman's characterization of conservatism, it is fascinating to note that Schumpeter may indeed be seen as advancing a kind of "futility thesis" as well—but, crucially, one aimed not at radical and progressive enemies but at putative conservative allies. He posited a futility due to flux, not permanence. Schumpeter argued conservatives must recognize that certain kinds of change were simply too powerful to halt. This viewpoint was linked, of course, to Schumpeter's historicism, his view that the backdrop to any adequate social or political theory is a reasoned account of ever-present tendencies toward change. As Sweezy pointedly summarized a key strand of Schumpeter's view: "capitalism is, like all social systems, a transitory phenomenon. It had a birth, it is now living its life, and sooner or later it will die" (Sweezy 1951, 121). This particular version of historicism is surely disagreeable for anyone who proposes to struggle against the currents of social and political change—the sort who, as William F. Buckley wrote memorably five decades ago, "stands athwart history, yelling Stop" (Buckley 1955, 5).[8] But it may be even more uncongenial to those who argue that any existing institution or system they favor, such as capitalism, taps uniquely into permanent and universal human proclivities. Finally, while we are on the subject of Schumpeter's deference to deep currents of historical change—albeit change of which he deeply disapproved—it is worth observing that this tenet has also simply resulted in his being badly misunderstood. It surely explains why Mommsen termed Schumpeter (quite erroneously) a "radical liberal with socialist tendencies" and why at least one reviewer termed him a socialist outright (Mommsen 1980, 21; Swedberg 1991b, 166).

Closely related to Schumpeter's rearguard conservatism was a set of attitudes characterizing his political communication—written and sometimes spoken—many of which may also make him difficult to embrace today. I refer here to habits of mind and argument that would discourage potential allies, no matter whether they were sought among conservatives, feminists, or socialists. (I only wish to address characteristics that emerge in and through what Schumpeter said and wrote, without attempting to found these traits on deeper psychological grounds.) First, there is a palpable gloom, an aroma of morbidity in some of Schumpeter's political writings that probably, in itself, repels. It emerged in the metaphor chosen when he wrote in 1928 that the capitalist "system" was not prone to crisis but that this was "no more sufficient as a basis for prediction than a doctor's diagnosis to the effect that a man has no cancer is a sufficient basis for the prediction that he will go on living indefinitely" (Schumpeter [1928] 1989, 71). And it surfaced notably again when he wrote: "Before humanity chokes (or basks) in the dungeon (or paradise) of socialism, it may well burn up in the horrors (or glories) of imperialist wars" (Schumpeter [1942] 1976, 163). But really this darkness pervaded much of Schumpeter's writings in a way that cannot be demonstrated by selective quotation. Mingled with this literary atmosphere was a kind of grim irony—not so much the use of literary irony by Schumpeter himself, but rather an appreciation, even a savoring, of historical irony. His sense that history played tricks on human beings, that things turned out quite differently from what they would rationally expect or intend was of course at the heart of Schumpeter's prediction that the "very success" of capitalism (61), chiefly its success in spreading rationalist habits of thought, would probably be its undoing. The quotation about the cancer prognosis—which I cited just above as an example of the morbid quality of Schumpeter's writings—is of course equally an illustration of this sense of historical irony with respect to the key problem of capitalist development. A less-appreciated example of historical irony in Schumpeter's writings is his view that while imperialism could not be blamed on capitalism in the way Lenin and Hilferding argued, nevertheless it could be attributed to the atavistic class that Schumpeter said was crucial to stabilizing and defending capitalism. In Schumpeter's narratives, of course, it was not always conservatives and pro-capitalists whose expectations were upended. For example, in 1918, he wrote that "Marx himself, if he lived today . . . would laugh grimly at those of his disciples who welcome the present administrative [war] economy as the dawn of socialism—that administrative economy which is the most undemocratic thing there is" (Schumpeter [1918] 1991, 130). Yet in his writings, both events, and irony itself, seem as often to wound Schumpeter's presumed allies. Consider a jab such as this, from *Capitalism, Socialism and Democracy*: "socialist democracy may eventually turn out to be more of a sham than capitalist democracy ever was" (Schumpeter [1942] 1976, 302). Here Schumpeter struck of course at those who hoped and predicted that socialism would be the true realization of democracy—but not without casually drawing blood from capitalist democrats as well.

Finally there can be found in Schumpeter four qualities of thought and expression so closely intertwined that it is difficult to say which one is in evidence at a given point in his writings. I refer to his pleasure in making others uncomfortable; his dexterity in adopting positions for the sake of argument; his apparent desire not to be taken for granted by any ideological camp; and his off-putting posture as someone who coolly proffered unpleasant truths. Take, for example, the story, repeated by several of his biographers, of Schumpeter's 1918 meeting with Max Weber at the Café Landmann across the *Ringstrasse* from the University of Vienna. According to a witness,[9] Schumpeter told Weber that he considered the Bolshevik revolution, of which both were critical, a "good laboratory to test our theories," and when Weber protested that the laboratory would be "heaped with human corpses" Schumpeter replied that this was no different from an "anatomy classroom." After more heated conversation, Weber stalked out, crying "this is intolerable!" But Schumpeter merely smiled to a companion and asked: "How can someone carry on like that in a coffee house?"[10] By comparison to this cool affrontery, Schumpeter's twin written pronouncements in

Capitalism, Socialism and Democracy—"Can capitalism survive? No. I do not think it can" ([1942] 1976, 61) and "Can socialism work? Of course it can" ([1942] 1976, 167)—may seem like only mild insults to the sensibilities of natural allies. More personally, we have Schumpeter's lashing out at Hayek as someone who "deals with ideas and principles as if they floated in the air"—one of several public accusations of naiveté in the same review (Schumpeter 1946, 270). Finally we have Schumpeter's habitual and determined treating of Marx with respect, indeed as "one of the most learned [economists] who ever lived" (Schumpeter [1949] 1989, 305). No matter how much he also criticized Marx, this ostentatious respect is bound to irritate not just conservatives of various varieties but also many liberals as well.

Schumpeter's anti-Semitic and pro-Nazi comments have probably also prevented at least some conservatives from embracing him. In 1992, not long after the appearance of Allen's intellectual biography (the first to give serious attention to those comments from Schumpeter's diary) Bernard Semmel published a piece in the conservative journal, *The Public Interest,* titled "Schumpeter's Curious Politics" (1992). Much of the article was devoted to a review of Allen's compelling evidence on the subject, which Semmel said provided "cause for sadness" (Semmel 1992, 4). Beyond this summary and comment, Semmel's approach was an illustration of the many difficulties some contemporary thinkers have had in digesting Schumpeter. For Semmel blended Schumpeter's anti-Semitism and pro-Nazi statements, his respectful treatment of Marx's intellect, and his reluctant forecasts of capitalist decline in *Capitalism, Socialism and Democracy* into a single betrayal of classical liberalism. In any case, it does seem likely that the anti-Semitic and pro-Nazi revelations may have deterred some conservatives from making use of Schumpeter during the past fifteen to twenty years. Whether they will continue to have that effect is uncertain. Thomas McCraw's recent intellectual biography deals with the evidence of anti-Semitism in an extended footnote that ends this way: "To me the evidence indicates that Schumpeter did have his prejudices . . . but that anti-Semitism was not one of these prejudices" (McCraw 2007, 511–12 n. 12).[11] Probably because of McCraw's focus on the Schumpeterian theme of innovation, his book was quickly noticed in conservative journals, whose reviewers did not mention the issue of anti-Semitism.[12]

* * *

Another consideration that has likely inhibited scholars and public intellectuals of all stripes from making use of Schumpeter is the fact that he seems to have been quite wrong about his forebodings about capitalism and socialism. But this ought to be far less of a hindrance to engaging with Schumpeter than it might appear to be. Schumpeter was always careful about "prediction." His forebodings were so spectacular that they have attracted more attention than the cautionary words attached to them. But the caveats were always there. In *Capitalism, Socialism and Democracy*, Schumpeter insisted:

> Analysis, whether economic or other, never yields more than a statement about the tendencies present in an observable pattern. And these never tell us what *will* happen to the pattern but only what *would* happen if they continued to act as they have been acting in the time interval covered by our observation and if no other factors intruded. (Schumpeter [1942] 1976, 61)

And this statement represents a good deal more than equivocation or bet-hedging by Schumpeter. It articulates something profound about the special problems of social science, which studies situations or sets of relations that are by definition open to many more mechanisms and forces than we can study at any given time, as well as to changes in the way those mechanisms operate. Not only do we never observe a single social mechanism or property at work—but those mechanisms or properties themselves may change as institutions, practices, and ideas change. For this reason, many theorists including Schumpeter have argued, social science should be precisely about the identification of the tendencies and properties of social systems, not about predicting how these tendencies will work out in the future.[13] While many social scientists continue to believe that prediction and explanation are coextensive, Schumpeter argued that a perfectly good and accurate explanation of how a particular institution, system or social relation works may give us no ability to predict future events at all. And many of the scholars who have turned their attention to *Capitalism, Socialism and Democracy's* "predictions" note precisely that Schumpeter should be evaluated and criticized for his analysis of tendencies, such as the institutionalization of innovation.[14]

And this brings us back to something I believe is at the heart of the matter: critically analyzing Schumpeter's view of the tendencies that characterized modern social and political development. For none of the features of Schumpeter's thought that may in fact inhibit some contemporary social theorists from drawing on him, interesting and significant though these they may be, prove that he is not relevant today. Neoconservatives, liberal democrats and socialists, admirers of Schumpeter and critics alike, all may find him relevant, if they remain conscious of the differences between his needs and purposes and theirs, if they engage critically with his views of such issues as the development of tax states, the sociology of intellectuals, or the rational capacities of voters. Especially when a thinker is as fertile as Schumpeter, neither flaws nor dissonances with our way of thinking are necessarily hindrances—they are positive provocations. There is still much to be written about how Schumpeter succeeded and failed in the many fields in which he made contributions, what he understood and misunderstood, analyzed and neglected—all in light of his underlying vision and his deepest political commitments.

Notes

1 Life

[1] We must not take this German identification to be something absolute or primordial. The family can be traced back to "Václav Šumpeter" who moved to Triesch in 1478 (Shionoya 1989, 159). Taylor (1942, 17) points out that there was a common process by which families of Czech (or Slovenian or Polish) peasants would become Germanized through moving to towns and taking up trade.

[2] Background on Triesch and Schumpeter's family there may also be found in McCraw (2007, ch. 1), Meissner (1979), Shionoya (1989), and Swedberg (1991b, ch. 1).

[3] Swedberg (1991b) reproduces a fragment of the prospective novel, *Ships in Fog*, as an appendix to his intellectual biography.

[4] Both Böhm-Bawerk's contribution and Hilferding's response may be found in a single volume: Böhm-Bawerk (1975).

[5] After Hitler's seizure of power, Hilferding had gone into exile in France. In February, 1941, contrary to promises given him and a fellow Social Democrat, Rudolf Breitscheid, Vichy authorities in Arles handed the two men over to the Nazis. During his first night in Gestapo custody, in accordance with a long-standing plan for such circumstances, Hilferding took an overdose of sleeping pills and died the next morning (Smalldone 1998, 205–7).

[6] Translated in Stolper (1994, 193). For the original German, see Schumpeter ([1916–18] 1992, 366).

[7] Translated in Stolper (1994, 180). For the original German, see Schumpeter ([1916] 1985, 271).

[8] No one who has read the memos can fail to register their intrinsic interest, but the usual approach to them suggests that they reflect only on a famous economist's personal beliefs and short-lived political ambitions. I have argued elsewhere that they prefigure his most highly praised writings on democracy (Medearis 2001, ch. 2), but this is not the accepted interpretation.

[9] See also: Medearis (2001, 65–6).

[10] For accounts of Schumpeter's term as finance minister, see: Allen (1991, 1: ch. 9), März (1981), Stolper (1994, 215–93), and Swedberg (1991b, 58–63).

[11] Schumpeter's and Reisinger's relationship is recounted in Allen (1991, 1: 192–8, 221–9), Swedberg (1991b, 72–5), and McCraw (2007, 113–24, 134–40).

[12] For differing assessments of the significance of this essay, especially for understanding Schumpeter's democratic theory, see: Medearis (2007, 57–64) and Zassenhaus (1981).

[13] After briefly sharing power with the Christian Social Party, during the period when Schumpeter was finance minister, the Austrian SDP went into more-or-less permanent opposition nationally, while enjoying overwhelming support in Vienna. Support for the Christian Socials was equally strong in the provinces, and Austria settled into a long period of stalemate punctuated by violent clashes between paramilitary forces tied to each bloc. The right-wing *Heimwehr* paramilitaries put increasing pressure on Christian Socials to expand executive power and limit democracy. The Christian Social government of Engelbert Dollfuss used a legislative fracas in 1933 as an excuse to close parliament and rule by decree, a practice that was, in any case, more to Dollfuss's advantage, since he lacked a majority in parliament. Ruling instead with the support of the right-wing *Heimwehr* and the Italian Fascist regime of Benito Mussolini, Dollfuss faced increasing demands from both to crush the Social Democrats. The opportunity came in early 1934, when, without the approval of party leaders, members of the socialist paramilitary *Schutzbund* in Linz took to arms to resist a police weapons search. Calls for a general strike were generally unheeded, but the fighting spread to Vienna, where government forces, fighting alongside *Heimwehr* units, fired artillery on working-class housing projects. After the *Schutzbund's* defeat, Dollfuss first banned the Social Democratic Party, then imposed a new constitution that gave him dictatorial powers and that ushered in what is frequently and justifiably termed "Austrofascism." Dollfuss's alliance with Mussolini and seizure of power, however, only put off the threat from a different opposition, the Nazis, very briefly. Dollfuss himself was killed in a Nazi coup a few months later. And forcible annexation by Nazi Germany took place in March, 1938. For less condensed accounts of these events, see: Gulick (1948), Jelavich (1987).

[14] Schumpeter's seven years as a professor at the University of Bonn (1925–32) were actually interrupted by two lengthy visits to Harvard University, during the academic years of 1927–8 and 1930–1.

[15] Translated in Allen (1991, 1: 285). For the original German, see Schumpeter ([1932] 1952, 606).

[16] For accounts of the Depression and New Deal, and especially the aspects that worried Schumpeter, see Bernstein (1970), Kennedy (1999), and Leuchtenberg (1963).

[17] It was replaced by the National Labor Relations Act, signed by Roosevelt in 1935, and upheld by the Supreme Court in 1937.

[18] This is excluding a 1915 pamphlet on the history of the social sciences.

[19] To a sentence of *Capitalism, Socialism and Democracy* reading "[b]efore humanity chockes (or basks) in the dungeon (or paradise) of socialism it may well burn up in the horrors (or glories) of imperialist wars" Schumpeter appended a footnote reading: "Written in the summer of 1935" (Schumpeter [1942] 1976, 163, 163 n. 6). But the first real outline of the book may date to 1939 (Allen 1991, 2: 88).

[20] Stöckel eventually married a Serbian economist and moved to Novi Sad, Yugoslavia where, in 1942, apparently because she was a member of the local English Club, she was shot by the Hungarian forces that ruled the city for the Nazis. For accounts of Schumpeter's relationship with her, see Allen (1991, 1: 233–5, 293–4; 2: 3, 12–13, 176) and McCraw (2007, 167, 189–91, 203, 233–5, 279–301). McCraw reproduces a series of her letters to Schumpeter.

[21] For accounts of their courtship and marriage, see Allen (1991, 2: 18, 46–7, 102–4, 109–10, 219–20), McCraw (2007, 235–43, 302–3, 337–44, 412–13), and Swedberg (1991b, 121–4, 142–3).

[22] See, for example: Allen (1991, 2: 91, 101, 113 n. 21) and Swedberg (1991b, 146).

[23] Schumpeter may have meant Carl Schmitt, the Nazi legal scholar who had been a fellow faculty member at Bonn.

[24] For accounts of his death, see Allen (1991, 2: 239), McCraw (2007, 488), and Swedberg (1991b, 193).

2 Critical Exposition

[1] For more on differences between Schumpeter and Hayek, see Chapter 4.

[2] Translated in: Swedberg (1991b, 29). For the original, see Schumpeter (1908, 567).

[3] The best-known critique of the approach is probably that by Hilferding, which may be found in Böhm-Bawerk (1975).

[4] Although emphasizing the concrete figure of the entrepreneur has value heuristically at this stage of the discussion, Schumpeter came to conclude that innovation could take place without the entrepreneur.

[5] The next paragraph draws on chapter IV of *Business Cycles*, "The contours of economic evolution" (Schumpeter 1939).

[6] While these three were discernible, Schumpeter thought, he was actually agnostic about how many superimposed cycles "really" existed.

[7] This argument echoes similar ones in both Hegel ([1821] 1991) and Marx ([1843] 2000).

[8] The term "princes" applies equally to any of the rulers of a class of jurisdictions within the Holy Roman Empire, including duchies and margraviates, but Schumpeter's discussion suggests most obviously the Holy Roman Emperor.

[9] Paul Sweezy argues (1951, 120 n. 7) that Schumpeter was "almost certainly unacquainted with Lenin's writings on imperialism" when he wrote his own essay, and points out that Lenin's work did not appear in German or French until 1920. And Service (1985, 2: 359 n. 94) confirms the publication history of Lenin's book.

[10] Or perhaps one should say: an alternative to what Schumpeter *took to be* a Marxist theory of class. Marx himself nowhere offered a definitive statement on class, central though the concept was to his work. In their famous anthology of class theories, Reinhard Bendix and Seymour Martin Lipset attempted to lay out the classic statements of eight social theorists, including Schumpeter and Marx. But in Marx's case, they were reduced to the expedient of excerpting a single page from an unfinished chapter of *Capital*, which they followed up with a six-page analysis in their own words (Bendix and Lipset 1966).

[11] See Schumpeter ([1916] 1985), Schumpeter (1920–1, 324–30), Schumpeter [(1918–19] 1991, 144–56), Schumpeter ([1927] 1991, 280), Schumpeter (1939, 304–14), Schumpeter ([1942] 1976, 134–239).

[12] To be precise, of course, Schumpeter distinguished between the second and third "Kondratieffs" or capitalist eras, the end of the second coming in 1897. Since he considered the sort of socio-political balance discussed here to be mainly a feature of the second "Kondratieff," one could say that he really only experienced this to the age of 14.

[13] This definition does not so much *solve* as *highlight* crucial problems, concerning the meaning and possible limits of intellectual autonomy, of logic and of empiricism. But serious discussion of these issues is beyond the scope of this chapter.

[14] It is perhaps a symptom of Schumpeter's greater ambivalence about rationality, as well, that "innovation" appears primarily as a good thing in Schumpeter's thought—especially in its home territory, capitalist enterprise—whereas it has a predominantly negative connotation for Burke.

[15] This may perhaps be admitted without arguing, as I have elsewhere (Medearis 2001), that Schumpeter had a "transformative" conception of democracy, in addition to his elite one.

[16] This characterization of human agency is so starkly negative that it has left some readers wondering whether Schumpeter's assumptions can coherently support even the minimal citizen participation and basic political liberties he described as features of an appropriately limited democracy. See Held (2006, 143, 153–4) and Medearis (2001, 124–7). Most interpreters, however, pass over these tensions, portraying Schumpeter's support for such minimal participatory mechanisms and basic liberties as unproblematic.

[17] For different versions of the argument that democracy and the protection of crucial rights mutually entail each other, see: Dahl (1985, 24–8), Habermas (1998), and Shapiro (1999, 20).

[18] Burke ([1774] 1999) makes a similar argument.

[19] For example, see Allen (1991, 2: 129–30).

[20] For example, see Bachrach (1967) and Ricci (1970).

[21] For an elaboration of this argument, see Medearis (2001, chs. 2, 3, and 4).

[22] It is possible to argue, as I have elsewhere (Medearis 2001, 133–9), that the vehemence of Schumpeter's case for elite domination of socialist democracy made for very strange bedfellows.

3 Influence

[1] Schumpeter's influence, of course, cannot be reduced to the influence of *Capitalism, Socialism and Democracy*. But for reasons I shall explain below, the story of its influence tells us much that we need to know about Schumpeter's broad influence as a social and political theorist.

[2] I am attempting here only to characterize the predominant frames or lenses through which it seems to me Schumpeter was read, especially in the English-speaking world. I do not mean to deny, for example, that the period was experienced differently in the developing world. Nor do I want to suggest that there was unanimity, even in the industrialized West, about the complacent assumptions at issue (there was not); or that existential fears disappeared there after 1945 (one need only mention the threat of nuclear annihilation); or that the apparent "exhausted consensus" signified that survivors of the Second World War had come to terms morally with what had transpired, most especially with genocide.

[3] Dahl (1961) provides a good summary of the movement's ambitions by a partisan. See also Farr (1995) and Ricci (1984).

[4] The dominant view of Schumpeter is of a tireless crusader for pure science as against politically or policy-oriented research, but I argue elsewhere (Medearis 2001, 167–6) that this is an oversimplification.

[5] And for the placement of "Schumpeterian" democracy in other typologies, see Gutmann (1993) and Shapiro (2003).

[6] See Kuznets (1940) and Lange (1941).

[7] Of course, in many fields, such as political science, there has been a countervailing tendency to adopt methods from mainstream economics.

[8] Schumpeter also stressed the importance of "frankly historical work," "industrial monographs," and "biographies of individual business leaders" in a letter to an economist in 1944 (Schumpeter 2000, 349–51).

[9] See, for example, Dosi et al. (1988) and Nelson and Winter (1982).

[10] For helpful surveys, see Birch (1984) and Held (2006, 172–9, 190–201).

[11] Perhaps precisely because such arguments about democracy had entered into the mainstream of political science, Huntington and his colleagues were inconsistent in citing Schumpeter, although they did cite him (Crozier et al. 1975, 6, 8).

[12] For overviews, see Bush (2006), Chilcote (2000), Etherington (1982), and Wolfe (1997).

[13] Of course, Schumpeter did write about premodern, non-Western imperialism, such as Egyptian and Assyrian imperialism.

[14] See, for example, Thompson (1966).

[15] Actually Schumpeter wrote not of "conveyances" but wrote more vividly of "a hotel or an omnibus" ([1927] 1991, 248).

[16] For example, see Edgell (1993), Joyce (1995), Scase (1992), and Wright (2005).

4 Relevance

[1] The Congress of Berlin (1878) was organized by Otto von Bismarck and staved off war by the partitioning of the Ottoman Empire.

[2] I have argued more pointedly elsewhere (Medearis 2001, ch. 5) that not just Schumpeter's political science heirs but Schumpeter himself can be criticized from the standpoint of his mature methodological viewpoint, and that Schumpeter's elite conception denied what he himself often recognized, that democracy was itself transformative, not merely a static system.

[3] See, for example, Sowell (2006).

[4] Using an electronic database to sample articles in prominent English-language conservative outlets during the most recent

decade, I found about 50 per cent more references to Strauss than to Schumpeter; more than four times as many references to Hayek; more than five times as many references to Rand; about seven times as many references to Burke; and almost eight times as many references to Friedman. I do not wish, however, to make a fetish of these figures, offering them cautiously and only as emblematic. The journals surveyed were prominent ones, but the list was not exhaustive. And the measure used—essentially instances of a thinker's name—is fairly undiscriminating. Moreover, since different magazines are indexed in different databases for different time periods, meaningful cross-magazine comparisons could not be made.

[5] And see Morris (1989). Despite these high profile appreciations, though, Schumpeter is still referred to less often in such business and economics publications than Friedman—and, in some cases, less often than Hayek. For provisos about such comparisons, see note 4 above.

[6] This is not to say that conservatives themselves have never tried. "Any informed conservative is reluctant to condense profound and intricate intellectual systems to a few pretentious phrases; he prefers to leave that technique to the enthusiasm of radicals," wrote Russell Kirk, a few sentences before listing "six canons of conservative thought" to which he claims conservatives have adhered "with a consistency rare in political history" (Kirk 1953, 7–8).

[7] And see McCraw (2007, 339–40).

[8] If the ambition to stand athwart history typified one conservative outlook in 1955, it is worth noting how different the outlook of some contemporary conservatives appears to be. The publisher of an encyclopedia of American conservatism recently boasted to a reporter: "We've gone from history's adversary to destiny's child" (DeParle 2006, A1).

[9] The next few sentences draw on the firsthand account of Felix Somary (1986, 120–1).

[10] Somary, who witnessed this exchange, considered Weber as responsible for the incident as Schumpeter.

[11] That summary judgment is somewhat modified by McCraw's review of other evidence he considers more "damning" (2007, 585–6 n. 44 and 586 n. 45).

[12] See Schulz (2007) and Kosar (2007).

[13] See, for example, Sayer (1992, ch. 4).

[14] See, for example, the contributions by Tom Bottomore, Gottfried Haberler, and Robert L. Heilbroner in Heertje (1981).

Bibliography

Works by Schumpeter

Schumpeter, J. A. (1908), *Das Wesen und der Hauptinhalt der theoretischen Nationalökonomie*. Berlin: Duncker & Humblot.

—([1911] 1934), *The Theory of Economic Development: An Inquiry into Profits, Capital, Credit, Interest and the Business Cycle*. Cambridge: Harvard University Press.

—([1916] 1985), "Memorandum I," in W. F. Stolper and C. Seidl (eds.), *Aufsätze zur Wirtshaftspolitik*. Tübingen: J. C. B. Mohr.

—([1916–18] 1992), "Schumpeters Briefe an Graf Otto Harrach," in C. Seidl and W. F. Stolper (eds.), *Politische Reden*. Tübingen: J. C. B. Mohr.

—([1918] 1991), "The crisis of the tax state," in R. Swedberg (ed.), *The Economics and Sociology of Capitalism*. Princeton: Princeton University Press, pp. 99–140.

—([1918–19] 1991), "The sociology of imperialisms," in R. Swedberg (ed.), *The Economics and Sociology of Capitalism*. Princeton: Princeton University Press, pp. 141–219.

—(1920–1), "Sozialistische Möglichkeiten von heute," *Archiv für Sozialwissenschaft und Sozialpolitik*, 48, 305–60.

—([1927] 1991), "Social classes in an ethnically homogenous environment," in R. Swedberg (ed.), *The Economics and Sociology of Capitalism*. Princeton: Princeton University Press, pp. 230–83.

—([1927] 1989), "The explanation of the business cycle," in R. V. Clemence (ed.), *Essays on Entrepreneurs, Innovations, Business Cycles, and the Evolution of Capitalism*. New Brunswick, NJ: Transaction, pp. 21–46.

—([1928] 1989), "The instability of capitalism," in R. V. Clemence (ed.), *Essays on Entrepreneurs, Innovations, Business Cycles, and the Evolution of Capitalism*. New Brunswick, NJ: Transaction, pp. 47–72.

—([1932] 1952), "Das Woher und Wohin unserer Wissenschaft," in E. Schneider and A. Spiethoff (eds.), *Aufsätze zur ökonomischen Theorie*. Tübingen: J. C. B. Mohr, pp. 598–608.

—(1934), "Depressions," in *The Economics of Recovery Program*. New York: McGraw-Hill.

Schumpeter, J. A. ([1937] 1989), "Preface to Japanese edition of 'Theorie der wirtschaftlichen Entwicklung'," in R. V. Clemence (ed.), *Essays on Entrepreneurs, Innovations, Business Cycles, and the Evolution of Capitalism.* New Brunswick, NJ: Transaction, pp. 165–8.

—(1939), *Business Cycles: A Theoretical, Historical, and Statistical Analysis of the Capitalist Process,* 2 vols. New York: McGraw-Hill.

—([1941] 1991), "An economic interpretation of our time: the Lowell lectures," in R. Swedberg (ed.), *The Economics and Sociology of Capitalism.* Princeton: Princeton University Press, pp. 339–400.

—([1942] 1947), "Preface," in *Capitalism, Socialism and Democracy,* 2nd edn. New York: Harper & Row.

—([1942] 1976), *Capitalism, Socialism and Democracy,* 3rd edn. New York: Harper & Row.

—([1945] 1991), "The future of private enterprise in the face of modern socialistic tendencies," in R. Swedberg (ed.), *The Economics and Sociology of Capitalism.* Princeton: Princeton University Press.

—(1946), Rev. of *The Road to Serfdom,* by F. A. Hayek. *The Journal of Political Economy,* 54, 3 (June), 269–70.

—([1949] 1989), "The Communist Manifesto in sociology and economics," in R. Clemence (ed.), *Essays on Entrepreneurs, Innovations, Business Cycles and the Evolution of Capitalism.* New Brunswick, NJ: Transaction.

—(1951), *Ten Great Economists, From Marx to Keynes.* Oxford: Oxford University Press.

—([1954] 1994), *History of Economic Analysis,* ed. E. B. Schumpeter. Oxford: Oxford University Press.

—(1970), *Das Wesen des Geldes,* ed. F. K. Mann. Göttingen: Vandenhoeck & Ruprecht.

—(2000), *Briefe/Letters,* ed. U. Hedtke and R. Swedberg. Tübingen: Mohr Siebeck.

Works by Other Authors

Allen, R. L. (1991), *Opening Doors: The Life and Work of Joseph Schumpeter,* 2 vols. New Brunswick, NJ and London: Transaction.

Arena, R., and C. Dangel-Hagnauer (2002), *The Contribution of Joseph Schumpeter to Economics: Economic Development and Institutional Change.* London: Routledge.

Augello, M. M. (1991), "Works by Schumpeter," in R. Swedberg (ed.), *Joseph A. Schumpeter: The Economics and Sociology of Capitalism.* Princeton: Princeton University Press, pp. 445–81.

Bachrach, P. (1967), *The Theory of Democratic Elitism, A Critique.* Boston: Little, Brown.

Backhaus, J. (2002), "Fiscal sociology: what for?," *American Journal of Economics and Sociology*, 61, 1, 55–77.

Baran, P. (1957), *The Political Economy of Growth.* New York: Monthly Review Press.

Barreto, H. (1989), *The Entrepreneur in Microeconomic Theory: Disappearance and Explanation.* London: Routledge.

Baumol, W. J. (1968), "Entrepreneurship in economic theory," *The American Economic Review*, 58, 2, 64–71.

Bell, D. (1960), *The End of Ideology: On the Exhaustion of Political Ideas in the Fifties.* Glencoe, IL: Free Press.

—(1976), *The Cultural Contradictions of Capitalism.* New York: Basic Books.

Bendix, R. (1951), Rev. of *Imperialism and Social Classes*, by J. A. Schumpeter. *American Journal of Sociology*, 57, 2, 198–200.

Bendix, R., and S. M. Lipset, eds. (1966), *Class, Status and Power: Social Stratification in Comparative Perspective*, 2nd edn. New York: Free Press.

Berelson, B., P. Lazarsfeld, and W. McPhee (1954), *Voting.* Chicago: University of Chicago Press.

Bernstein, I. (1970), *Turbulent Years: A History of the American Worker, 1933–1941.* Boston: Houghton Mifflin.

Birch, A. H. (1984), "Overload, ungovernability and delegitimation: the theories and the British case," *British Journal of Political Science*, 14, 135–60.

Böhm-Bawerk, E. (1975), *Karl Marx and the Close of His System*, by Eugen von Böhm-Bawerk, and *Böhm-Bawerk's Criticism of Marx*, by Rudolf Hilferding. Reprints of Economic Classics. Clifton, NJ: Augustus M. Kelley.

Bonney, R. (1999), "Introduction," in R. Bonney (ed.), *The Rise of the Fiscal State in Europe, c. 1200–1815.* Oxford: Oxford University Press.

Bottomore, T. B. (1966), *Classes in Modern Society.* New York: Pantheon Books.

—(1992), *Between Marginalism and Marxism: The Economic Sociology of J. A. Schumpeter.* New York: St. Martin's Press.

Braun, R. (1975), "Taxation, sociopolitical structure, and state-building: Great Britain and Brandenburg-Prussia," in C. Tilly (ed.), *The Formation of National States in Western Europe.* Princeton: Princeton University Press.

Brewer, J. (1989), *The Sinews of Power: War, Money and the English State, 1688–1783.* London: Unwin Hyman.

Brownlee, W. E. (1996), "Reflections on the history of taxation," in W. E. Brownlee (ed.), *Funding the Modern American State, 1941–1995.* New York: Woodrow Wilson Center Press and Cambridge University Press.

Buckley, W. F. (1955), "Publisher's statement," *National Review.* November 19, 1955, p. 5.

Burke, E. ([1790] 1999), "Reflections on the revolution in France," in I. Kramnick (ed.), *The Portable Edmund Burke.* New York: Penguin, pp. 416–74.

—([1774] 1999), "Speech at Mr. Burke's arrival in Bristol," in I. Kramnick (ed.), *The Portable Edmund Burke.* New York: Penguin, pp. 155–8.

Bush, B., (2006), *Imperialism and Postcolonialism.* Harlow: Pearson Longman.

Campbell, J. L. (1993), "The state and fiscal sociology," *Annual Review of Sociology,* 19, 163–85.

Chilcote, R. H. (2000), *Imperialism: Theoretical Directions.* Amherst, NY: Humanity.

Cole, G. D. H. (1952), Rev. of *Imperialism and Social Classes,* by J. A. Schumpeter. *The Economic Journal,* 62, 245, 177–80.

Crozier, M., S. P. Huntington, and J. Watanuki (1975), "Introduction," in M. Crozier, S. P. Huntington, and J. Watanuki (eds.), *The Crisis of Democracy.* New York: New York University Press.

Dahl, R. A. (1961), "The behavioral approach in political science: epitaph for a monument to a successful protest," *American Political Science Review,* 55, 4, 763–72.

—(1985), *Preface to Economic Democracy.* Berkeley and Los Angeles: University of California Press.

—(1989), *Democracy and Its Critics.* New Haven: Yale University Press.

Davis, H. B. (1951), Rev. of *Imperialism and Social Classes,* by J. A. Schumpeter. *Political Science Quarterly,* 66, 3, 465–66.

DeParle, J. (2006), "An A-to-Z book of conservatism now weighs in," *New York Times,* June 21, A1.

Dosi, G., C. Freeman, R. R. Nelson, G. Silverberg, and L. Soete, eds. (1988), *Technical Change and Economic Theory.* London: Pinter Publishers.

Downs, A. (1957), *An Economic Theory of Democracy.* New York: HarperCollins.

Drucker, P. F. (1983), "Schumpeter and Keynes, in which the author argues that our politicians and economists, sometimes unknowingly, are following the wrong prophet," *Forbes,* May 23, pp. 124–8.

Edgell, S., ed. (1993), *Class.* London: Routledge.

Etherington, N. (1982), "Reconsidering theories of imperialism," *History and Theory,* 21, 1, 1–36.

Farr, J. (1995), "Remembering the revolution: behavioralism in American political science," in J. Farr, J. S. Dryzek, and S. T. Leonard (eds.), *Political Science in History: Research Programs and Political Traditions*. Cambridge: Cambridge University Press, pp. 198–224.

Ferguson, N. (2003), *Empire: The Rise and Demise of the British World Order and the Lessons for Global Power*. New York: Basic.

Frank, A. G. (1969), *Capitalism and Underdevelopment in Latin America*. New York: Monthly Review Press.

Friedländer, S. (1997), *Nazi Germany and the Jews, Vol. I, The Years of Persecution, 1933–1939*. New York: Harper-Perennial.

Galbraith, J. K. (1977), Rev. of *Capitalism, Socialism and Democracy*, by J. A. Schumpeter. *New Society*, April 14, 1977, 74–5.

—(1981), *A Life in Our Times*. Boston: Houghton-Mifflin.

Giddens, A. (1973), *The Class Structure of the Advanced Societies*. London: Hutchinson University Library.

Gulick, C. A. (1948), *Austria, From Habsburg to Hitler*. 2 vols. Berkeley and Los Angeles: University of California Press.

Gutmann, A. (1993), "Democracy," in R. E. Goodin and P. Pettit (eds.), *A Companion to Contemporary Political Philosophy*. Oxford: Blackwell.

Haberler, G. (1950), "Joseph Alois Schumpeter, 1883–1950," *Quarterly Journal of Economics*, 64 (August 3), 333–84.

—(1981), "Schumpeter's Capitalism, Socialism and Democracy after forty years," in A. Heertje (ed.), *Schumpeter's Vision: Capitalism, Socialism and Democracy after Forty Years*. Eastbourne, East Sussex: Praeger.

Habermas, J. (1975), *Legitimation Crisis*. Boston: Beacon Press.

—(1998), "On the internal relation between the rule of law and democracy," in C. Cronin and P. D. Greiff (eds.), *The Inclusion of the Other: Studies in Political Theory*. Cambridge: MIT Press.

Hancock, W. K. (1952), Rev. of *Imperialism and Social Classes*, by J. A. Schumpeter. *International Affairs*, 28, 2, 196.

Hansen, A. H. (1936), Rev. of *The Theory of Economic Development: An Inquiry into Profits, Capital, Credit, Interest and the Business Cycle*, by J. A. Schumpeter. *Journal of Political Economy*, 44, 4, 560–3.

Harris, S. E., ed. (1951), *Schumpeter, Social Scientist*. Cambridge: Harvard University Press.

Hayek, F. A. (1939), *Freedom and the Economic System*, ed. H. D. Gideonse, Public Policy Pamphlet No. 29, Chicago: University of Chicago Press.

—([1944] 1994), *The Road to Serfdom*. Chicago: University of Chicago Press.

Hayek, F. A. (1959), *The Constitution of Liberty*. Chicago: University of Chicago Press.

—(1973–9), *Law, Legislation and Liberty*, 3 vols. Chicago: University of Chicago Press.

Heertje, A., ed. (1981), *Schumpeter's Vision: Capitalism, Socialism and Democracy after 40 Years*. Eastbourne, East Sussex: Praeger.

Hegel, G. W. F. ([1821] 1991), *Elements of the Philosophy of Right*, trans. H. B. Nisbet. Cambridge: Cambridge University Press.

Heilbroner, R. L. (1999), *The Worldly Philosophers: The Lives, Times, and Ideas of the Great Economic Thinkers*, 7th edn. New York: Touchstone-Simon & Schuster.

Held, D. (2006), *Models of Democracy*. Stanford: Stanford University Press.

Hilferding, R. (1975), "Böhm-Bawerk's criticism of Marx," in P. M. Sweezy (ed.), *Karl Marx and the Close of His System*, by Eugen von Böhm-Bawerk and *Böhm-Bawerk's Criticism of Marx*, by Rudolf Hilferding. Clifton, NJ: Augustus M. Kelley, pp. 123–224.

Hirschman, A. O. (1991), *The Rhetoric of Reaction*. Cambridge: Belknap-Harvard University Press.

Hobsbawm, E. J. (1994), *The Age of Extremes: A History of the World, 1914–1991*. New York: Vintage.

Hobson, J. (1997), *The Wealth of States: A Comparative Sociology of International Economic and Political Change*. Cambridge: Cambridge University Press.

Howey, R. S. (1935), Rev. of *The Theory of Economic Development: An Inquiry into Profits, Capital, Credit, Interest and the Business Cycle*, by J. A. Schumpeter. *American Economic Review*, 25, 1, 90–1.

Huntington, S. P. (1975), "The United States," in M. Crozier, S. P. Huntington, and J. Watanuki (eds.), *The Crisis of Democracy*. New York: New York University Press, pp. 59–118.

Jelavich, B. (1987), *Modern Austria: Empire and Republic, 1815–1986*. Cambridge: Cambridge University Press.

Johnson, C. A. (2000), *Blowback: The Costs and Consequences of American Empire*. New York: Metropolitan.

Johnston, W. M. (1972), *The Austrian Mind: An Intellectual and Social History*. Berkeley and Los Angeles: University of California Press.

Joyce, P. ed., (1995), *Class*. Oxford: Oxford University Press.

Kennedy, D. M. (1999), *Freedom from Fear: The American People in Depression and War, 1929–1945*. New York: Oxford University Press.

Kirk, Russell (1953), *The Conservative Mind, from Burke to Santayana*. Chicago: Regnery.

Kirzner, I. M. (1973), *Competition and Entrepreneurship*. Chicago: University of Chicago.

Kosar, K. R. (2007), "Mr. Creative Destruction: Joseph Schumpeter and the truth about capitalism," *The Weekly Standard*, 12, 35 (April 23, 2008).

Kristol, W., and D. Brooks, (2000), "The politics of creative destruction; McCain's challenge to an ossified Republican establishment reveals the outlines of a potential governing majority," *The Weekly Standard*, March 13, p. 24. LexisNexis (April 21, 2008).

Kruger D. H. (1955), "Hobson, Lenin, and Schumpeter on Imperialism," *Journal of the History of Ideas*, 16, 2, 252–9.

Kuznets, S. (1940), "Schumpeter's business cycles," *The American Economic Review*, 30, 2, 257–71.

Lange, O. (1941), Rev. of *Business Cycles: A Theoretical, Historical and Statistical Analysis of the Capitalist Process*, by J. A. Schumpeter. *The Review of Economic Statistics*, 23, 4, 190–3.

Lans, A. (1944), Rev. of *Mobilizing for Abundance*, by R. R. Nathan, *Postwar Economic Problems*, by S. E. Harris, *Capitalism, Socialism and Democracy*, by J. A. Schumpeter, and *Where's the Money Coming From?*, by S. Chase. *Yale Law Journal*, 53, 4, 830–52.

Leuchtenberg, W. E. (1963), *Franklin Delano Roosevelt and the New Deal, 1932–1940*. New York: Harper Torchbooks.

Low, A. D. (1974), *The Anschluss Movement, 1918–1919, and the Paris Peace Conference*. Philadelphia: American Philosophical Society.

Marschak, J. (1940), Rev. of *Business Cycles: A Theoretical, Historical and Statistical Analysis of the Capitalist Process*, by J. A. Schumpeter. *The Journal of Political Economy*, 48, 6, 889–94.

Marx, K. ([1843] 2000), "On the Jewish question," in D. McLellan (ed.), *Karl Marx, Selected Writings*, 2nd edn. Oxford: Oxford University Press, pp. 46–70.

Marx, K., and F. Engels ([1848] 2000), "The Communist Manifesto," in D. McLellan (ed.), *Karl Marx, Selected Writings*, 2nd edn. Oxford: Oxford University Press, pp. 245–72.

Mãrz, E. (1981), "Joseph A. Schumpeter as minister of finance of the first republic of Austria, March 1919–October 1919," in H. Frisch (ed.), *Schumpeterian Economics*, Eastbourne, East Sussex: Praeger.

May, A. J. (1965), *The Hapsburg Monarchy, 1867–1914*. Cambridge: Harvard University Press.

—(1966), *The Passing of the Hapsburg Monarchy, 1914–1919* (2 vols.). Philadelphia: University of Pennsylvania Press.

Mayer, A. J. (1981), *The Persistence of the Old Regime: Europe to the Great War*. New York: Pantheon Book.

McCraw, T. K., ed. (1997), *Creating Modern Capitalism: How Entrepreneurs, Companies, and Countries Triumphed in Three Industrial Revolutions*. Cambridge: Harvard University Press.

McCraw, T. K. (2007), *Prophet of Innovation: Joseph Schumpeter and Creative Destruction*. Cambridge: Belknap Press of Harvard University Press.

Medearis, J. (2001), *Joseph Schumpeter's Two Theories of Democracy*. Cambridge: Harvard University Press.

Meissner, F. (1979), "The Schumpeters and the industrialization of Třešť'," *Zeitschrift für die gesamte Staatswissenschaft*, 135, 256–62.

Miller, J. J. (1999), "The 100 best non-fiction books of the century," *National Review*, Vol. 51, No. 8. LexisNexis (April 21, 2008).

Mommsen, W. J. (1980), *Theories of Imperialism*. New York: Random House.

Morris, Charles R. (1989), "The coming global boom: its prophet is Joseph Schumpeter, and signs of its times will be written in rising international production, falling interest rates, and propitious demographic patterns," *The Atlantic Monthly*, October, pp. 51–64.

Nelson, R., and S. Winter (1982), *An Evolutionary Theory of Economic Change*. Cambridge: Cambridge University Press.

Oakeshott, M. ([1947] 1991), "Rationalism in politics," in *Rationalism in Politics and Other Essays*. Indianapolis, IN: Liberty Fund.

Oakley, A. (1990), *Schumpeter's Theory of Capitalist Motion: A Critical Exposition and Reassessment*. Hants: Edward Elgar.

O'Connor, J. ([1973] 2004), *The Fiscal Crisis of the State*. New Brunswick, NJ: Transaction.

Offe, C. (1984), *Contradictions of the Welfare State*. Cambridge: MIT Press.

Pateman, C. (1970), *Participation and Democratic Theory*. Cambridge: Cambridge University Press.

Polanyi, K. ([1944] 2001), *The Great Transformation: The Political and Economic Origins of Our Time*. Boston: Beacon Press.

Ricci, D. M. (1970), "Democracy attenuated: Schumpeter, the process theory, and American democratic thought," *The Journal of Politics*, 32, 2 (May), 239–67.

—(1984), *The Tragedy of Political Science: Politics, Scholarship and Democracy*. New Haven: Yale University Press.

Robinson, J. (1943), Rev. of *Capitalism, Socialism and Democracy*, by J. A. Schumpeter. *The Economic Journal*, 53 (212), 381–3.

Roth, J. (1995), *The Radetzky March*. Woodstock, NY: Overlook Press.

Sacks, D. H. (1994), "The paradox of taxation: fiscal crises, parliament, and liberty in England, 1450–1640," in P. T. Hoffman and K. Norberg (eds.), *Fiscal Crises, Liberty, and Representative Government, 1450–1789*. Stanford: Stanford University Press.

Said, E. ([1978] 2003), *Orientalism*. London: Penguin.

Sayer, A. (1992), *Method in Social Science*, 2nd edn. London: Routledge.

Scase, R., ed. (1992), *Class*. Minneapolis: University of Minnesota Press.

Schmitter, P. C., and T. L. Karl (1996), "What democracy is . . . and is not," in L. Diamond and M. F. Plattner (eds.), *The Global Resurgence of Democracy*. Baltimore: Johns Hopkins University Press.

Schulz, N. (2007), Rev. of *Prophet of Innovation: Joseph Schumpeter and Creative Destruction*, by T. K. McCraw. *National Review*, July 9. LexisNexis (April 21, 2008).

Seidl, C. (1984), "Joseph Alois Schumpeter: character, life and particulars of his Graz period," in C. Seidl (ed.), *Lectures on Schumpeterian Economics*. Berlin: Springer-Verlag.

Semmel, B. (1992), "Schumpeter's curious politics," *The Public Interest*, 106, 3–16.

Service, R. (1985), *Lenin, A Political Life*, "Worlds in collision, Vol. 2," Bloomington: Indiana University Press.

Shapiro, I. (1999), *Democratic Justice*. New Haven: Yale University Press.

—(2003), *The State of Democratic Theory*. Princeton: Princeton University Press.

Shionoya, Y. (1989), "The Schumpeter family in Třešt'," *Hitotsubashi Journal of Economics*, 30, 157–71.

—(1997), *Schumpeter and the Idea of Social Science: A Metatheoretical Study*. Cambridge: Cambridge University Press.

Smalldone, W. (1998), *Rudolf Hilferding, The Tragedy of a German Social Democrat*. Dekalb: Northern Illinois University Press.

Somary, F. (1986), *The Raven of Zurich: The Memoirs of Felix Somary*, trans. A. J. Sherman. London: C. Hurst & Co.

Sowell, T. (2006), *On Classical Economics*. New Haven: Yale University Press.

Stolper, W. F. (1985), "Schumpeter and the German and Austrian socialization attempts of 1918–1919," *Research in the History of Economic Thought and Methodology*, 3, 161–85.

—(1994), *Joseph Alois Schumpeter: The Public Life of a Private Man*. Princeton: Princeton University Press.

Sundbo, J. (1998), *The Theory of Innovation: Entrepreneurs, Technology and Strategy*. Cheltenham: Edward Elgar.

Swedberg, R. (1989), "Joseph A. Schumpeter and the Tradition of Economic Sociology," *Journal of Institutional and Theoretical Economics*, 145, 508–24.

—(1991a), "The man and his work," in R. Swedberg (ed.), *The Economics and Sociology of Capitalism*. Princeton: Princeton University Press, pp. 3–98.

—(1991b), *Schumpeter: A Biography*. Princeton: Princeton University Press.

Sweezy, P. M. (1943), "Professor Schumpeter's theory of innovation," *Review of Economic Statistics*, 25, 1, 93–6.

Sweezy, P. M. (1951), "Schumpeter on imperialism and social classes," in S. E. Harris (ed.), *Schumpeter, Social Scientist*. Cambridge: Harvard University Press, pp. 119–24.

Sweezy, P. M., M. Dobb, K. Takahashi, R. Hilton, C. Hill, G. Lefebvre, G. Procacci, E. Hobsbawm, and J. Merrington (1976), *The Transition from Feudalism to Capitalism*. London: NLB.

Taylor, A. J. P. (1942), *The Habsburg Monarchy, 1815–1918*. London: Macmillan.

Thompson, E. P. (1966), *The Making of the English Working Class*. New York: Vintage.

Urbinati, N. (2006), *Representative Democracy*. Chicago: Chicago University Press.

Wallerstein, I. M. (1974–89), *The Modern World-System*, 3 vols. New York and London: Academic Press.

Whalen, C. J. (2000), "Today's hottest economist died 50 years ago," *Business Week*, December 11. LexisNexis (June 24, 2008).

Wolfe, A. B. (1943), Rev. of *Capitalism, Socialism and Democracy*, by J. A. Schumpeter. *Political Science Quarterly*, 58, 2, 265–7.

Wolfe, P. (1997), "History and imperialism: a century of theory, from Marx to postcolonialism," *The American Historical Review*, 102, 2, 388–420.

Wright, D. M. (1951), Rev. of *Imperialism and Social Class*, by J. A. Schumpeter. *Southern Economic Journal*, 18, 1, 98.

Wright, E. O., ed. (2005), *Approaches to Class Analysis*. Cambridge: Cambridge University Press.

Zassenhaus, H. K. (1981), "The 'vision' and the 'theories'," in A. Heertje (ed.), *Schumpeter's Vision: Capitalism, Socialism and Democracy after Forty Years*. Eastbourne, East Sussex: Praeger.

Index